# Harvest Bountiful Trading Profits Using Andrews Pitchfork

## Price Action Trading With 80% Accuracy

Bryan V Post

ISBN-13 (print): 978-1-7354946-0-9
ISBN-13 (digital): 978-1-7354946-1-6

Library of Congress Control Number: 2020915337

Cover image: American Gothic, painting by Grant Wood

Published by Satori Traders LLC in
San Diego, California, United States of America

# ABOUT THE AUTHOR

Bryan became interested in trading the financial markets after attending a get-rich-quick seminar about automated trading software.

Although he knew almost nothing about trading at the time, he did know how to recognize and walk away from people selling snake-oil.

The seminar piqued Bryan's interest, however, and over the next few years he:

- absorbed innumerable books  about how to trade

- attended numerous online and live courses on trading

- attempted to swing trade and day trade profitably

- developed and tested automated trading strategies

- donated money to the markets repeatedly

Learning how to use Andrews Pitchfork from Timothy Morge marked the turning point in Bryan's path to consistent profitability as a trader.

Over subsequent years Bryan enhanced his trading success by adding Fibonacci tools and elements of Elliott Wave principle to the elegant simplicity of Andrews Pitchfork strategy.

# INTRODUCTION

Regardless of our Trading strategy or the time frame in which we choose to trade, we all have to answer the same question when sitting down to look at price charts:

"What is going on with this market and how do I trade it profitably?"

Day trading, Swing trading, Position trading, Trend following—our strategy for interacting with the financial markets doesn't matter.

Regardless of what we are trying to accomplish in the markets, we need to first figure out what price is doing.

Technical indicators may help with this task, but they always lag the price action, give conflicting trading signals, and can quickly lead to the dreaded paralysis of analysis.

What we need is a reliable method for accurately predicting where price will go <u>in the future</u>.

There are only two predictive technical analysis methodologies: Andrews Pitchfork strategy and Fibonacci techniques.

Some market technicians will argue that Elliott wave principle is also predictive in nature. I would counter that Elliott wave theory is more of an art form than a science.

Part I of this book focuses specifically on Andrews Pitchfork.

If you are an experienced Forker, this section of the book will serve as a quick review of basic principles and the five Andrews Pitchfork rules.

If you are new to Andrews Pitchfork, welcome! Forks are the most powerful tool you can put in your trading toolkit, bar none. Part I will serve as your primer.

The second half of the book is about understanding price behavior: what price is doing now and what it is likely to do in the future.

Within this context of interpreting price action, two predictive Fibonacci techniques are presented.

By integrating the techniques in Part I and Part II a trader can build a framework within which they can apply their entry/exit strategies and money/risk management techniques.

Old pros and newbies alike will find value in this book.

Keep on Forking!

# TABLE OF CONTENTS

## PART I—ANDREWS PITCHFORK

# PART II—TECHNICAL ANALYSIS

# PART I

## ANDREWS PITCHFORK

# NEWTON / BABSON / ANDREWS / MORGE

## ISAAC NEWTON

Isaac Newton (1642-1727) was a British physicist and mathematician who formulated the laws of motion and gravity. His third law of motion, "For every action there is an equal and opposite reaction", intrigued Roger Babson who studied the law in depth and applied it to price behavior in the financial markets.

## ROGER BABSON

Roger Babson (1875-1967) was an accomplished entrepreneur and businessman in the first half of the 20th century.

In 1904 he pioneered the financial services industry by founding Babson's Statistical Organization to analyze stocks, bonds and business reports. This analysis was published in newsletter form for Wall Street investment firms and individuals.

He established Babson College in Massachusetts in 1919. The school offered a unique curriculum combining academics with hands-on business training. The majority of the school's faculty was businessmen instead of academicians. Today the College is highly ranked world-wide for teaching entrepreneurship at both the graduate and undergraduate levels.

Babson was publicly credited with accurately forecasting the crash of 1929.

He was a prolific writer who authored more than 40 books on economic and social matters as well as magazine articles and newspaper columns. He also lectured on business and financial trends.

Babson amassed a $50 million fortune by applying Newton's third law to price behavior. He taught these "Action – Reaction" techniques to Alan Andrews.

## ALAN HALL ANDREWS

Dr. Alan H. Andrews (??–1985) was a thermodynamics professor at MIT.

After retiring he taught the 'Andrews Action Reaction' seminar and published a weekly newsletter. The materials from his course are dated in the 1960's and 1970's. One of the techniques he taught was the Pitchfork.

Andrews publicly stated that his work was based on Roger Babson's "Action – Reaction" work from the 1930's. The two men had met at a trading seminar and become friends. Andrews named his seminar the Action Reaction Course in acknowledgement of Babson's teachings.

## TIMOTHY MORGE

Dr. Andrews taught a few students in his own home and, as a young man, Timothy Morge (1958-2020) was fortunate enough to be one of those people. With this early foundation in trading and market knowledge Timothy built a highly successful career as a professional trader, ultimately accumulating nearly 40 years of experience trading and mentoring other traders.

Timothy was a consummate educator. He was a regular lecturer at MIT, Stanford and the University of Chicago (where he earned three PhD's in Math, Physics, and Economy). He also mentored 100's of professional traders and hedge fund managers privately while educating the wider trading community through his websites, articles and group mentoring sessions.

Timothy described the Andrews Pitchfork as, "the single most powerful tool in my trading tool kit", and strived to pass Andrews' teachings on to others.

# DRAWING AN ANDREWS PITCHFORK

What's the best way to define an Andrews Pitchfork? Let's draw one and we can develop our definition as we go along.

Chart 1. A blank chart that we want to analyze

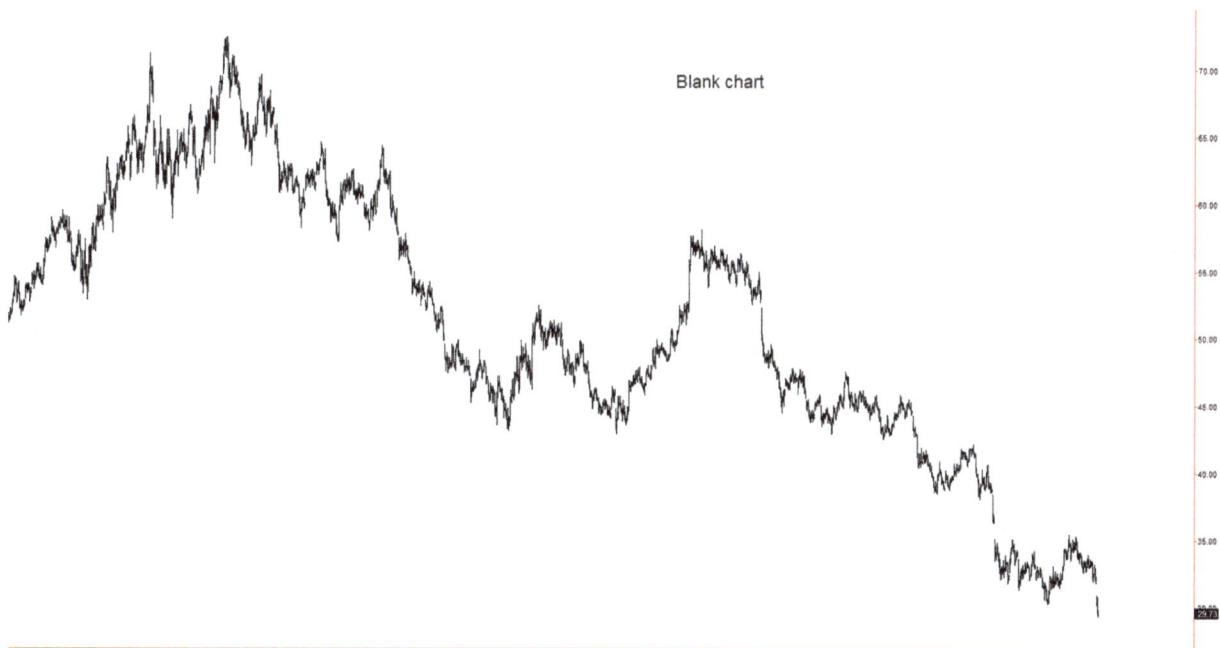

Blank chart

full-size chart available at https://satoritraders.com/andrews-pitchfork/charts

It is obvious in this particular chart that we are looking at a downtrend. To apply an Andrews Pitchfork when price is falling we need a sequence of high-low-high price pivots so we will pick the three points labeled in Chart 2. In an uptrend we would look for a significant low-high-low sequence.

## Chart 2. High-Low-High price sequence

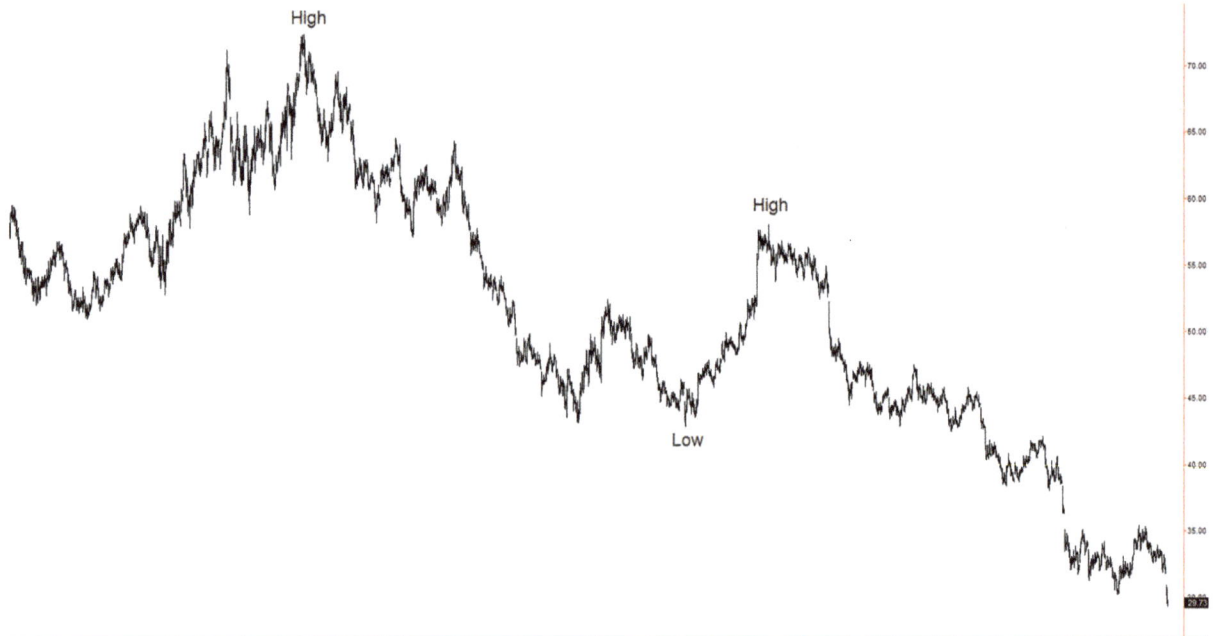

In Chart 3 we draw a line between the Low and High points of the High-Low-High sequence and find the mid-point or median of that line.

## Chart 3. Midpoint (or Median) of the line

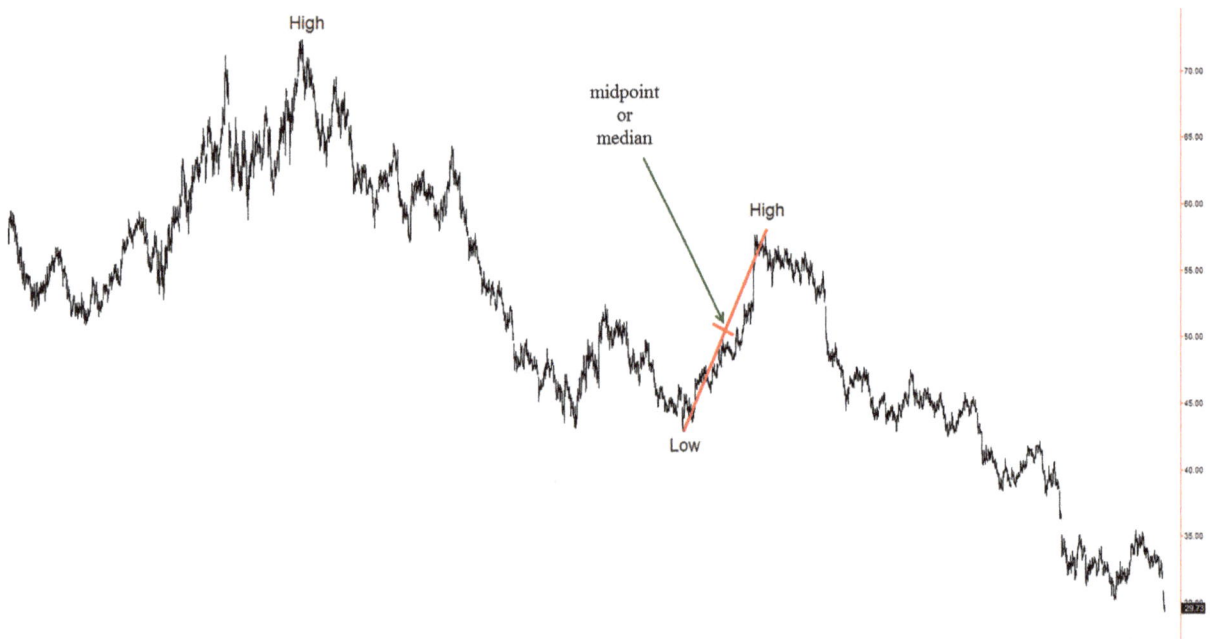

Using the first High point of the three-pivot sequence as our starting point, we draw a line through the midpoint identified in Chart 3. The result is the blue median line shown in Chart 4.

## Chart 4. Median Line (ML)

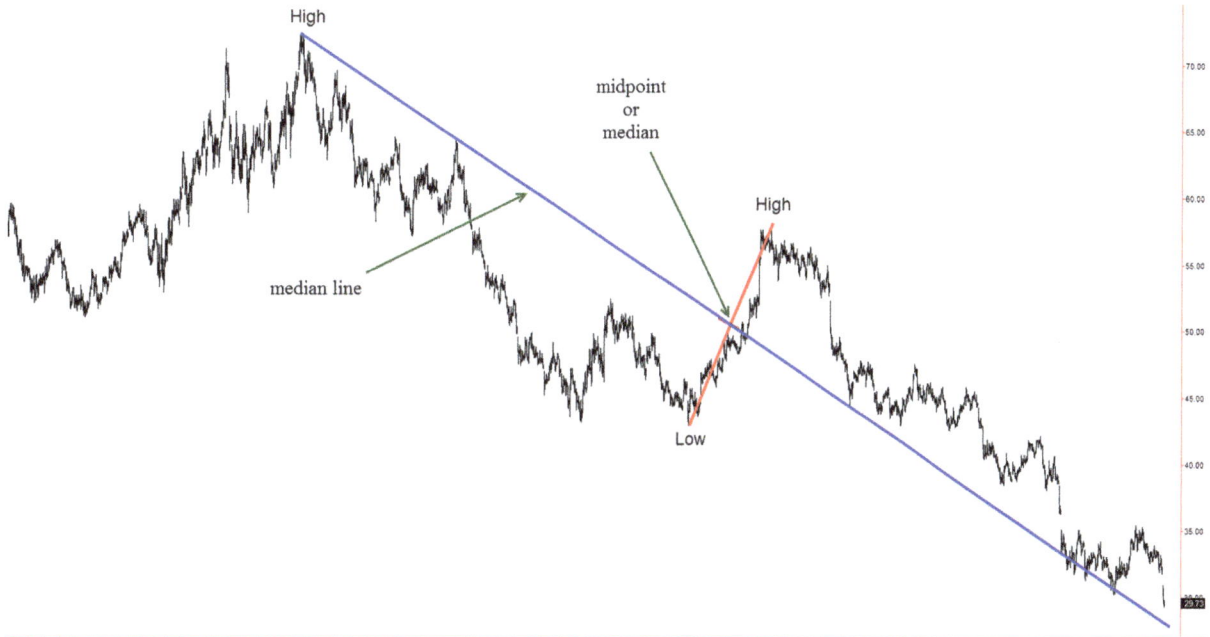

full-size chart available at https://satoritraders.com/andrews-pitchfork/charts

In Chart 5 we draw two lines that are parallel to the median line and place their origins at the Low and High pivot points. These parallel lines become the upper and lower median lines of the Andrews Pitchfork.

## Chart 5. Median Line parallels

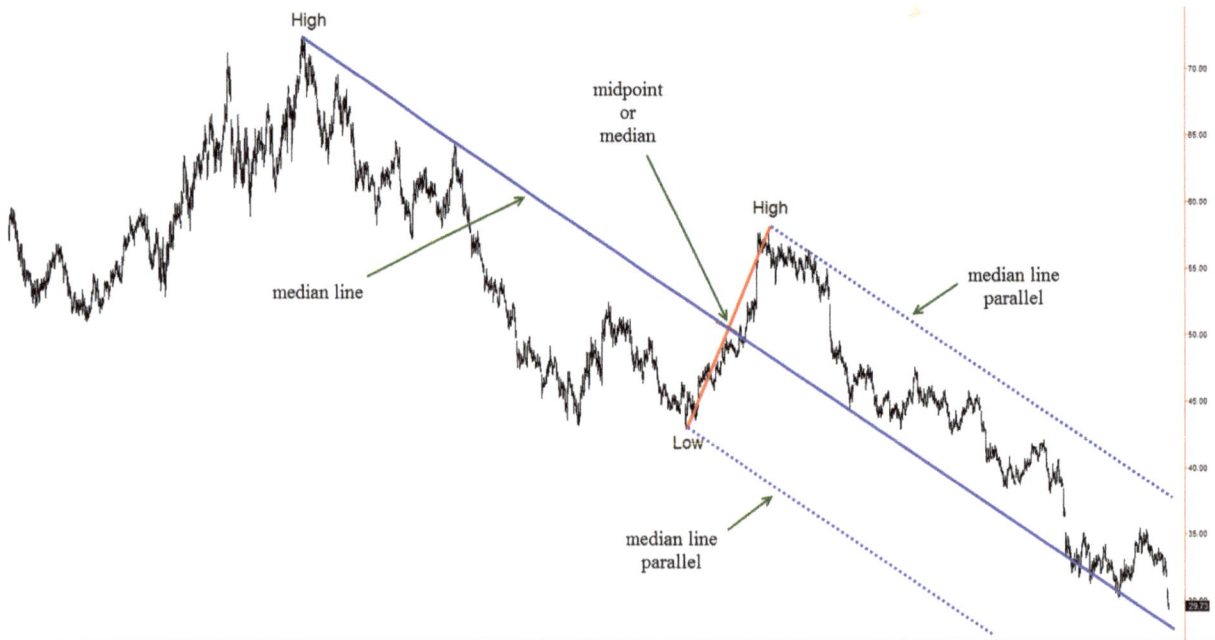

full-size chart available at https://satoritraders.com/andrews-pitchfork/charts

Most charting packages include the Andrews Pitchfork tool so we don't have to follow this multi-step process of drawing the median line and its parallels. Using our charting package we draw an Andrews Pitchfork as shown in Chart 6.

## Chart 6. Andrews Pitchfork

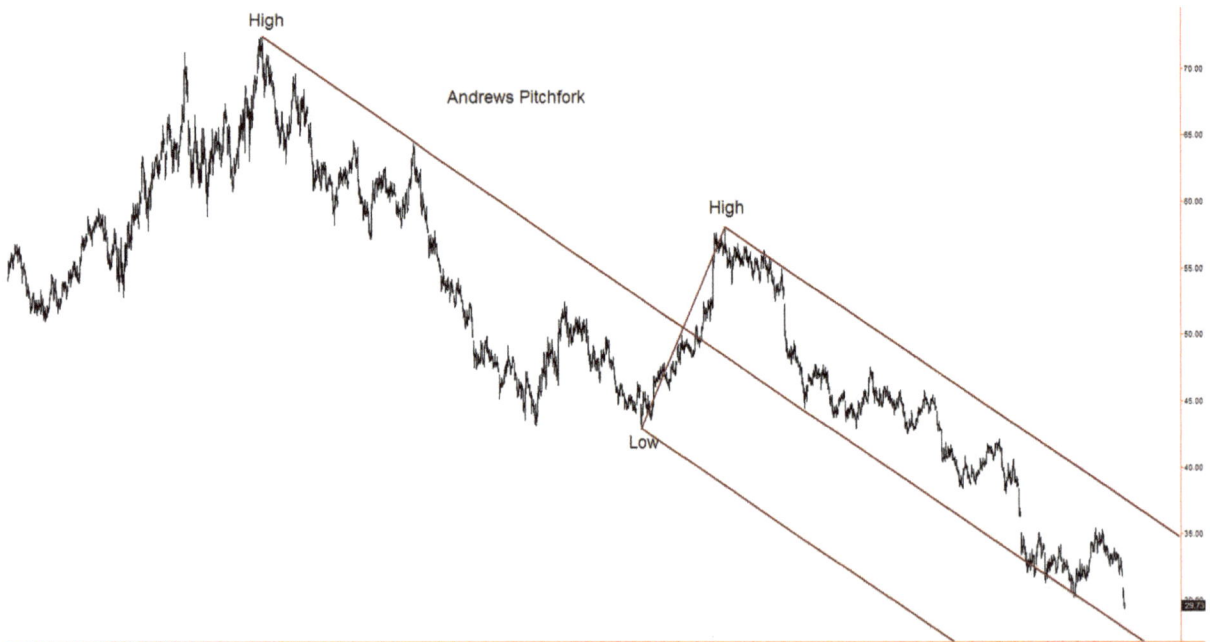

full-size chart available at https://satoritraders.com/andrews-pitchfork/charts

Not all forks are created equal.

Before we make any price projections based on a fork we need to assess its quality or validity. To do so we look for interactions between price and the fork lines. In Chart 7 we have highlighted these interactions.

Chart 7. Assessing fork quality

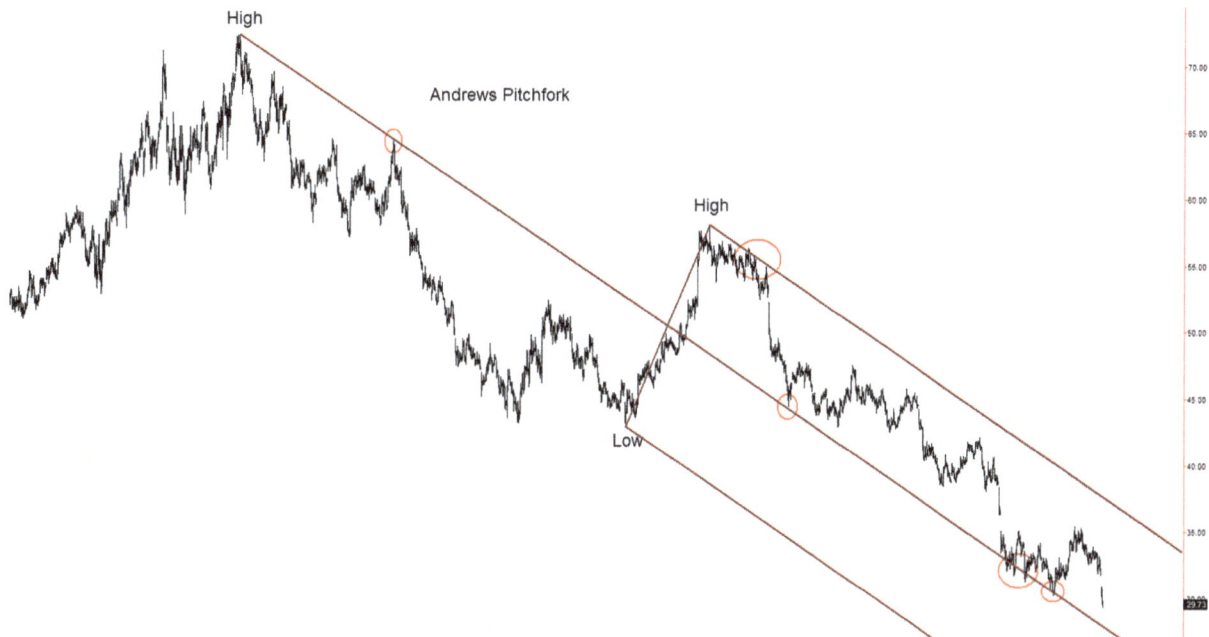

full-size chart available at https://satoritraders.com/andrews-pitchfork/charts

The Pitchfork in Chart 7 is describing price action quite well so we could say that it is 'proven' or 'valid'.

When we have a proven fork it is reasonable to expect that price will continue to react at the median lines of that fork until price action proves otherwise.

In general, the more a fork's median lines are tested for support/resistance the more confidence we can have that the fork will continue to influence price behavior.

# HOW DO WE USE IT?

According to Andrews price will reach the median line of a pitchfork 80% of the time. With this piece of information we can look for opportunities to get long near a swing low or short near a swing high and use the median line of the pitchfork as our profit target.

Let's pretend that we are watching a market with the intention of getting short. When the series of high-low-high price pivots form we draw a tentative Andrews Pitchfork as shown in Chart 1 and continue watching the price action.

Chart 1. Tentative Andrews Pitchfork

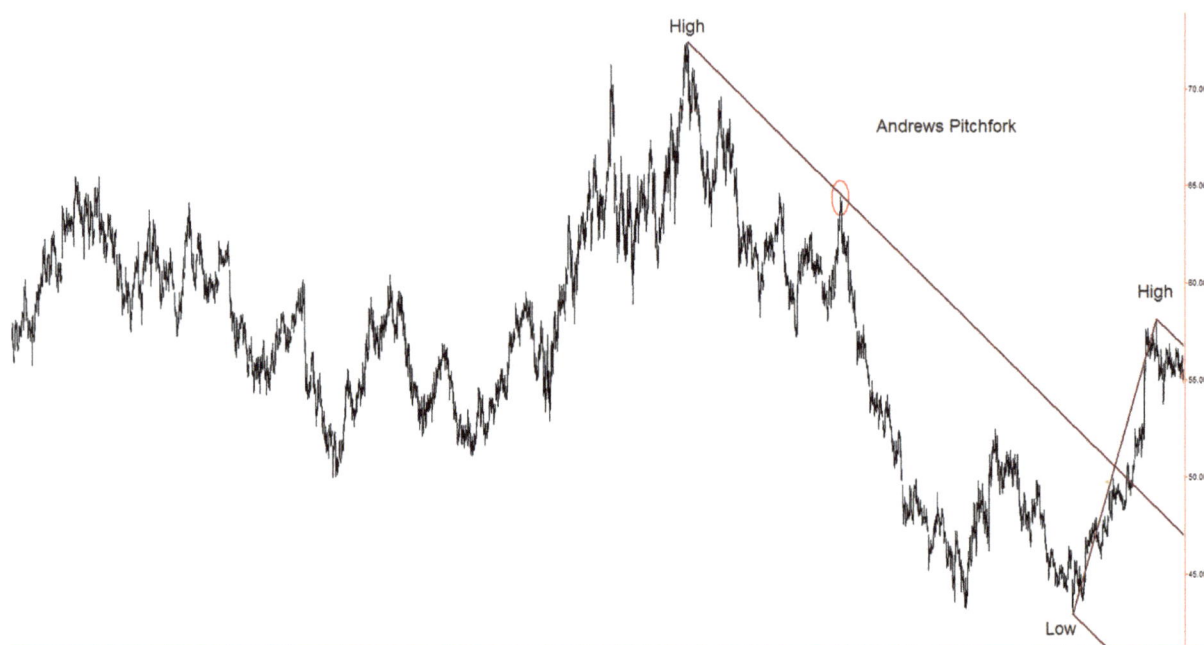

full-size chart available at https://satoritraders.com/andrews-pitchfork/charts

In Chart 2 price tests the upper median line three separate times giving us additional confirmation that we are working with a valid fork. Depending on our trading strategy we might get short at any one of those three tests. Being conservative we could use the first test as a confirmation of the pitchfork and still have two opportunities to get short.

This strategy of entering the market near a swing point allows us to use tight stops and predict our risk-to-reward ratio. If we were trading Chart 2 we might enter an order to sell short at $55.00 with a stop-loss order above the high at $58.00. We would use the fork's median line as our profit target to estimate our potential gain on the trade. In this case the median line is around $45.00 so we have a potential $10.00 gain against a potential $3.00 loss giving us a ratio of better than 3:1.

If the size of the stop-loss and the risk-to-reward ratio fit within our trading plan we can pull the trigger and execute the trade. If the trade parameters don't fit our trading plan we can keep our capital safe while looking for better trades. Both alternatives are made possible using Andrews Pitchfork.

Chart 2. Possible short entry points

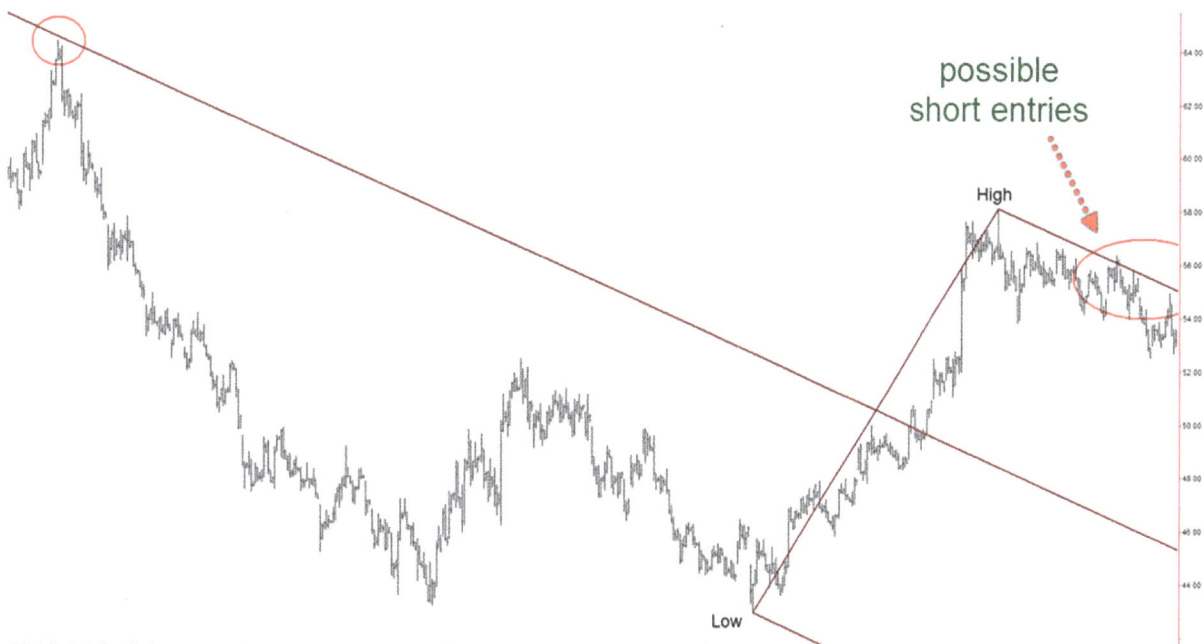

full-size chart available at https://satoritraders.com/andrews-pitchfork/charts

In Chart 3 we see that price did reach the median line of the pitchfork just like Andrews said would happen 80% of the time. In our hypothetical trade we would have an exit order placed just above the median line and we would move this order lower as time progressed.

Chart 3. Price will reach the median line 80% of the time

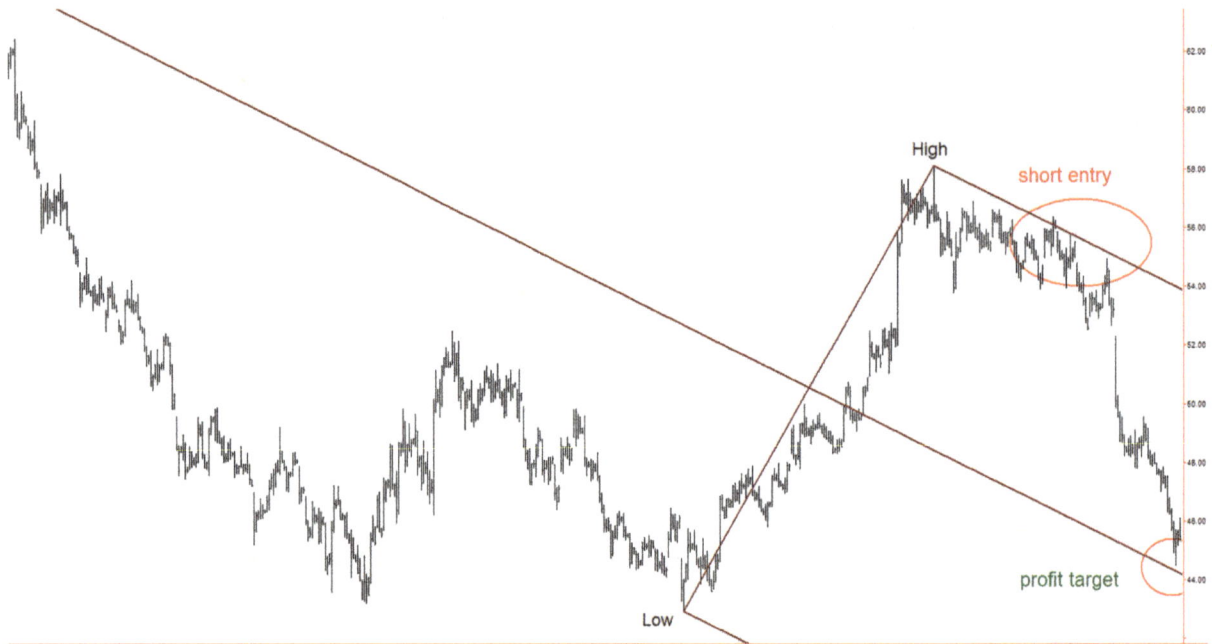

full-size chart available at https://satoritraders.com/andrews-pitchfork/charts

There are additional trading strategies for Andrews Pitchfork and we will explore them in other examples.

Besides providing specific trading strategies to implement, the Andrews Pitchfork tool allows us to unequivocally determine trend direction.

Look at Chart 4 and try to pretend that price is in an uptrend. The pitchfork makes it obvious, if it wasn't already, that price is trending downwards.

Whenever we draw a valid pitchfork in a trending market it will either be upwards-sloping or downwards-sloping so there will be no ambiguity about the trend. Whether we are trading with the trend or attempting to trade counter-trend, it is critical to accurately assess the trend in the time frame being traded. Andrews Pitchfork lets us do just that.

Chart 4. Andrews Pitchfork describing downtrend in price

full-size chart available at https://satoritraders.com/andrews-pitchfork/charts

# 5 RULES FOR USING ANDREWS PITCHFORK

There are five basic rules for using Andrews Pitchfork:

1. There is a high probability that price will reach the latest median line (ML)

2. Price will either reverse at the ML, gap (zoom) through it, or consolidate above/below it

3. When price passes through the ML, it will pull back and retest the ML before continuing

4. Price reverses at any ML or ML parallel

5. When price reverses before reaching the ML, it will move more in the opposite direction than when it was rising toward the ML (Hagopian's Rule)

**Rule 1**. There is a high probability that price will reach the latest median line (ML)

Rule 1 is demonstrated in Chart 1.

## Chart 1. Price drops to median line

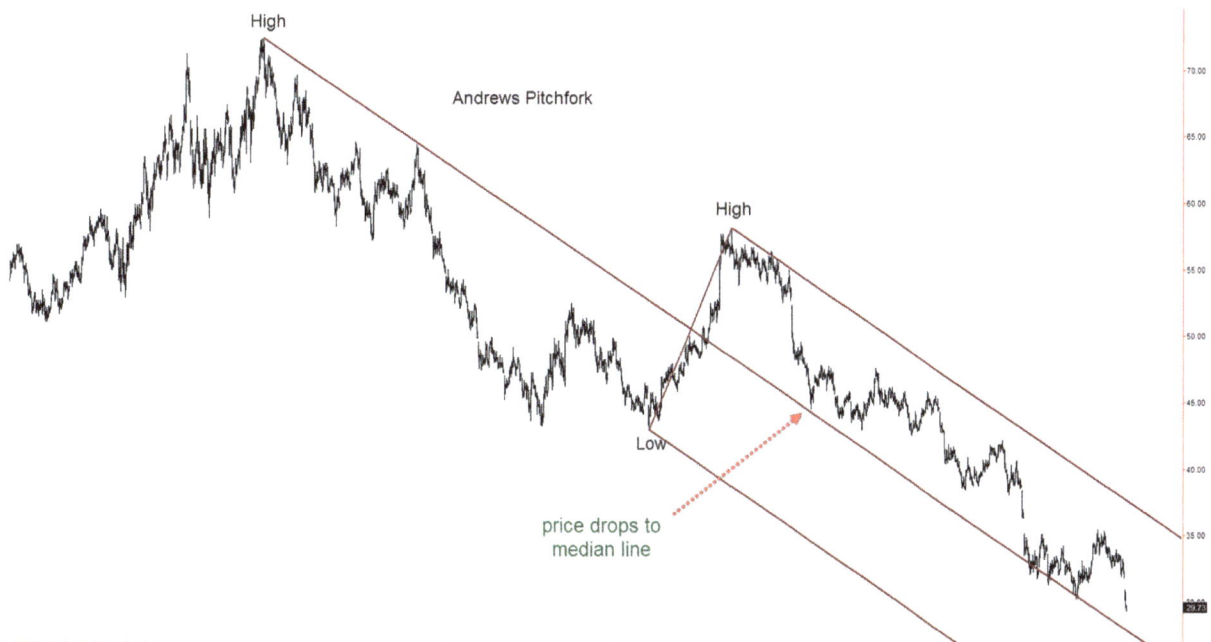

full-size chart available at https://satoritraders.com/andrews-pitchfork/charts

**Rule 2.** Price will either reverse at the ML, gap (zoom) through it, or consolidate above/below it

We see Rule 2 demonstrated in Chart 2 where price reaches the median line and then 'zooms' or accelerates through it.

**Rule 3.** When price passes through the ML, it will pull back and retest the ML before continuing

Rule 3 is also demonstrated in Chart 2 as price pulls back and retests the median line after zooming through.

## Chart 2. Price zooms the median line and retests

full-size chart available at https://satoritraders.com/andrews-pitchfork/charts

In Chart 3 we have a close-up look at the zoom and retest. After the zoom we have two retests where a nimble trader could get short for quick trades. When price pushes back above the median line these trades would get stopped-out if they were still open.

After price plunges back below the ML we get another opportunity to trade a retest of the fork's median line. When price tests the median line from below and gets rejected we have confirmation that the pitchfork is still influencing the price action so we place our entry order just below the median line and wait.

When price tests the median line again our order is executed and we are short this market with a tight stop placed just above the retest of the ML. As price declines we work our stop order lower and exit the trade just above the lower median line.

Chart 3. Zoom median line and retest—close up

full-size chart available at https://satoritraders.com/andrews-pitchfork/charts

In Chart 4 price reaches the median line and then gaps through before retesting the ML from below. In this particular pitchfork the price action is slightly offset from the fork's median line and price retests both the median line and the offset line after the zoom. As we saw in Chart 3 the retest of the median line gives us an opportunity to get short.

Chart 4. Gap through median line and retest

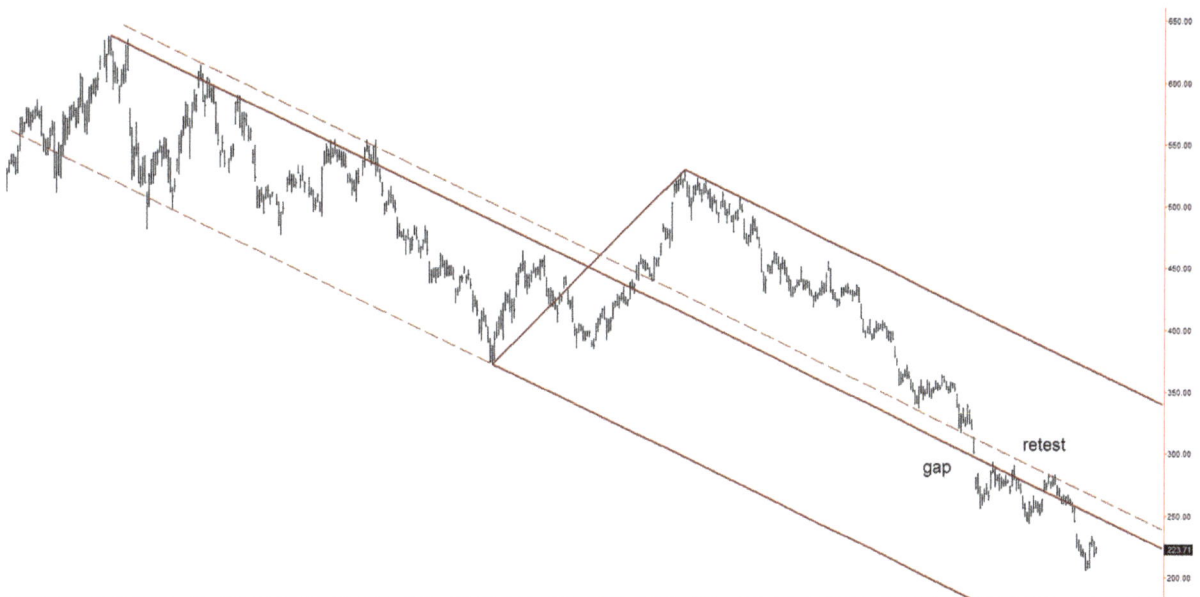

full-size chart available at https://satoritraders.com/andrews-pitchfork/charts

**Rule 4.** Price reverses at any ML or ML parallel

Price can reverse at the median line as we see in Chart 5. The reversal can also occur at the fork's upper or lower median line or at any of the median line parallels.

Chart 5. Price reverses at median line

price reaches median line
and then reverses

full-size chart available at https://satoritraders.com/andrews-pitchfork/charts

**Rule 5.** When price reverses before reaching the ML, it will move more in the opposite direction than when it was rising toward the ML (Hagopian's Rule)

When price fails to reach the median line of the current fork, Hagopian's Rule says that price will reverse and likely reverse with force. In Chart 6 we see a tentative Andrews Pitchfork that appears to have good quality. We could reasonably expect price to reach this fork's median line but it doesn't. When price reverses it does so with force and moves quickly lower.

## Chart 6. Hagopian's Rule

high

price fails to
reach median line

Hagopian's Rule in play

low

low

full-size chart available at https://satoritraders.com/andrews-pitchfork/charts

# STANDARD-SCHIFF PITCHFORK

Jeremy Schiff was a student of Andrews and he developed the Schiff Pitchfork based on his own observations.

The standard-Schiff Pitchfork is derived by moving the origin of an Andrews Pitchfork one-half (1/2) the vertical distance between the high and low points as shown in Chart 1.

### Chart 1. Standard-Schiff pitchfork

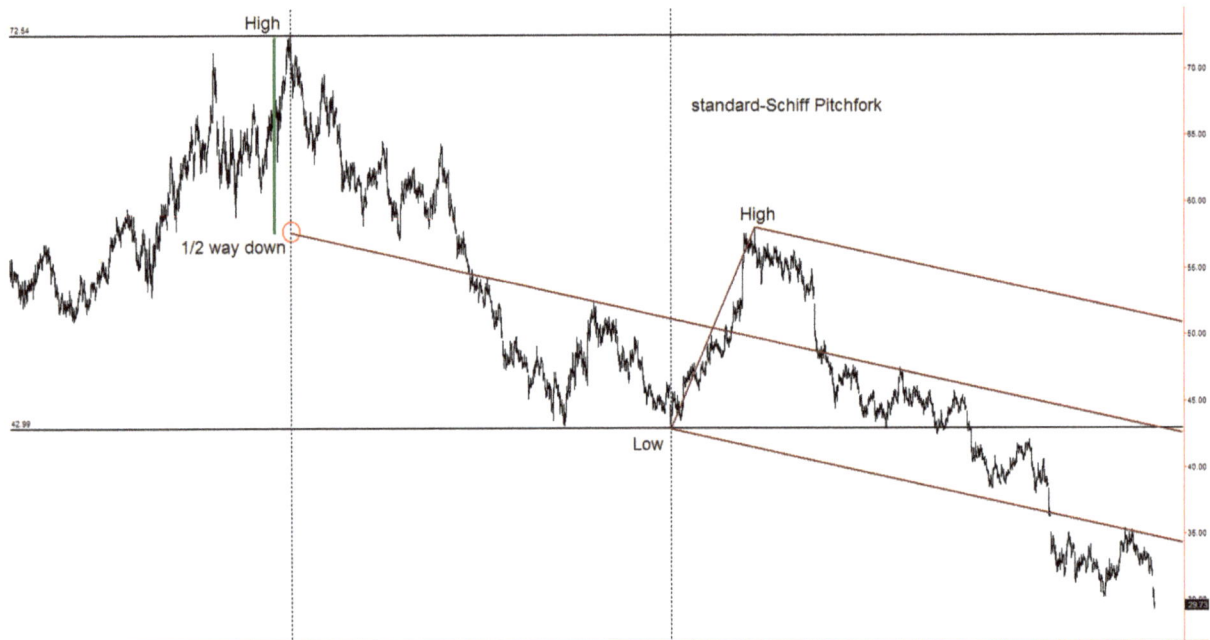

full-size chart available at https://satoritraders.com/andrews-pitchfork/charts

This standard-Schiff fork is describing price action quite nicely. In Chart 2 we highlight the interactions between price and the pitchfork lines. Notice that the Pitchfork identified several potentially profitable trades.

Chart 2. Price interacts with standard-Schiff pitchfork

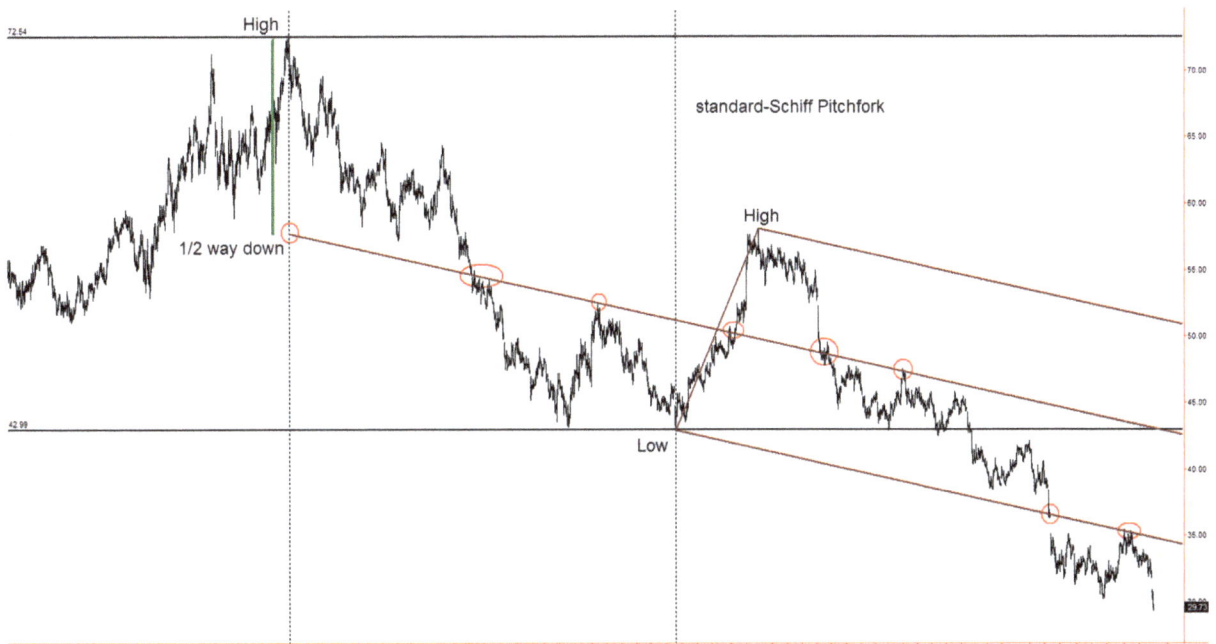

full-size chart available at https://satoritraders.com/andrews-pitchfork/charts

# MODIFIED-SCHIFF PITCHFORK

Schiff presented his pitchfork to Andrews and Andrews suggested a modification.

A modified-Schiff Pitchfork is derived by moving the fork's origin one-half (1/2) the vertical distance and one-half (1/2) the horizontal distance between the high and low as shown in Chart 1. The origin of the fork is now at the mid-point of the blue trend line drawn between the high and low points.

Chart 1. Modified-Schiff Pitchfork

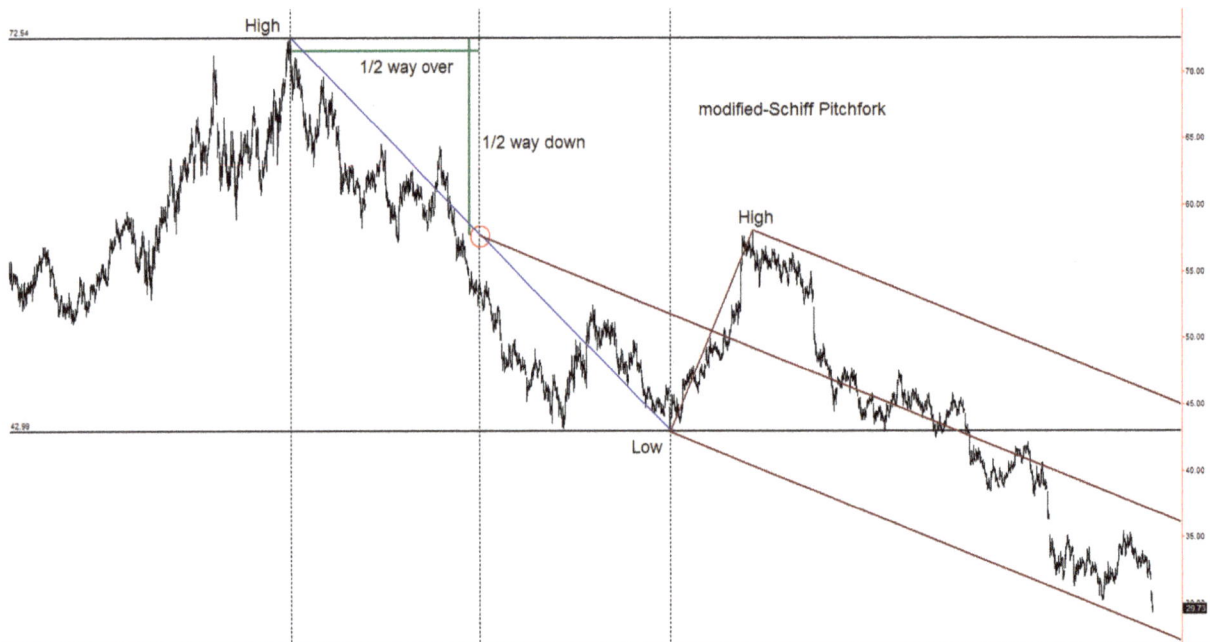

full-size chart available at https://satoritraders.com/andrews-pitchfork/charts

# PARALLEL LINES

Once we have a pitchfork drawn we can then draw lines which are parallel to the pitchfork's median line. Timothy Morge refers to them as 'sliding parallels' because we can slide them around on a chart. These parallels help us predict support/resistance areas and they further confirm the validity of the pitchfork as price interacts with them.

In Chart 1 we have a modified-Schiff Pitchfork describing a price uptrend. Price works higher within the fork and then overthrows the fork's upper median line in an exhaustion move. When this price spike ends we draw a sliding parallel on our chart at the level of the price peak. The sliding parallel marks a support/resistance level where price may run out of energy in the future.

As we can see in Chart 1, within a few trading sessions price makes another impulsive move higher but runs out of energy at the sliding parallel. If we are long during this rally the sliding parallel gives us a price target where we can exit or take partial profits. If we are looking for opportunities to get short we can wait for price to fail at the sliding parallel and then enter on a retest if it occurs.

The fact that price interacts with the sliding parallel a second time confirms that we have identified a valid pitchfork, and more importantly, that price is still being influenced by the fork. With this information we can continue executing our trading plan within the framework provided by the pitchfork.

## Chart 1. Sliding parallels

full-size chart available at https://satoritraders.com/andrews-pitchfork/charts

Besides being useful when used in conjunction with Andrews Pitchfork, parallel lines allow us to identify trading ranges and price channels (slanted trading ranges).

The first side of a trading range or price channel is typically drawn as a horizontal support/resistance line or a slanted trend line. We find the other side of the range by cloning the first line and moving the clone so it encompasses the current price action.

It isn't always possible to draw a pitchfork that accurately describes the price action in a chart. Sometimes applying the concept of parallel lines will identify opportunities to enter and exit a market.

## Chart 2. Trading ranges and price channels

Apple Inc, 1D, Cboe BZX

trading ranges / price channels

full-size chart available at https://satoritraders.com/andrews-pitchfork/charts

# FREQUENCY

By definition an oscilloscope "allows observation of constantly varying signal voltages". One of the measurements we can make with an oscilloscope is the frequency of the signal being monitored.

Now consider a price chart and imagine that it is the screen of an oscilloscope. Couldn't we measure the frequency of the price signal flowing through our test instrument? Of course we could.

In "Trading with Median Lines, Mapping the Markets", Timothy Morge states it this way: "For simplicity, I say the Median Line carries a specific frequency imparted by the relationship between its three pivots."

When we identify a valid Andrews Pitchfork we have found one of the frequencies which price is oscillating at. There may be multiple frequencies at play in any given chart and the specific frequencies are likely to vary between timeframes and trading vehicles.

This concept of frequencies in price charts helps explain why parallel lines are useful when using Andrews Pitchfork. A valid pitchfork identifies the frequency of price action in a given chart and all lines parallel to that fork have the same frequency and are therefore also valid.

# ENERGY

We have seen that an Andrews Pitchfork defines the trend for us. In a trending market a valid pitchfork will be either upward-sloping or downward-sloping. A fork can also help us determine when a market trend is running out of energy prior to a reversal.

In Chart 1 we see an Andrews Pitchfork describing the price action of a long-term uptrend. Look at the last three price peaks in the chart and notice that the first of these peaks occurred at the upper median line while each of the next two peaks occured further away from this line.

This failure of price to reach the upper median line is a sign that the trend is running out of energy and we can see in the chart that price subsequently dropped to the fork's median line and fell through.

# Chart 1. Price losing energy

Price is losing energy within this
Andrews Pitchfork

High

Low

Low

full-size chart available at https://satoritraders.com/andrews-pitchfork/charts

# ANDREWS TO MODIFIED-SCHIFF TRANSITION

One of the few truisms we can apply to the financial markets is that trends change.

A strong trend eventually loses energy and becomes a gentle trend. The gentle trend loses energy and price reverses direction or waffles sideways.

Using Andrews Pitchfork and the fork variations we can track these changing trends as they occur.

In Chart 1 we see price trending upwards with an Andrews Pitchfork describing the action. Price reaches the fork's median line just as Andrews predicted and then works its way higher along the median line. This price move eventually runs out of energy and drops back to the lower median line in search of support.

After finding support along the fork's lower median line, price charges higher again but runs out of energy before reaching the median line of the fork. The failure to reach the fork's median line serves as a signal that price behavior may be changing.

## Chart 1. Price losing energy in Andrews Pitchfork

full-size chart available at https://satoritraders.com/andrews-pitchfork/charts

When price moves out of an Andrews Pitchfork, the modified-Schiff version of that same pitchfork will oftentimes describe the subsequent price action. In Chart 2 the original Andrews Pitchfork is drawn with dotted lines and the modified-Schiff version with solid lines.

Notice how price interacts with the median line and lower median line of the modified-Schiff fork. While trending gently higher within the lower channel of this fork, price rallies towards the median line and reaches it on the second attempt.

After this peak, price rolls over and drops quickly to the fork's lower median line (ML). The lower ML provides support momentarily, but energy continues to wane and price makes a decisive move lower.

## Chart 2. Price rolls over into modified-Schiff Pitchfork

full-size chart available at https://satoritraders.com/andrews-pitchfork/charts

After price runs out of energy in the modified-Schiff pitchfork we can start looking for downward sloping forks. In Chart 3 we see an Andrews Pitchfork describing a new downtrend.

## Chart 3. Price begins a downtrend

full-size chart available at https://satoritraders.com/andrews-pitchfork/charts

# TERMINOLOGY

In Chart 1 we have labeled the lines in an Andrews Pitchfork to provide a common terminology for reference.

The median line parallels are also referred to as median line extensions.

Chart 1. Naming the parts

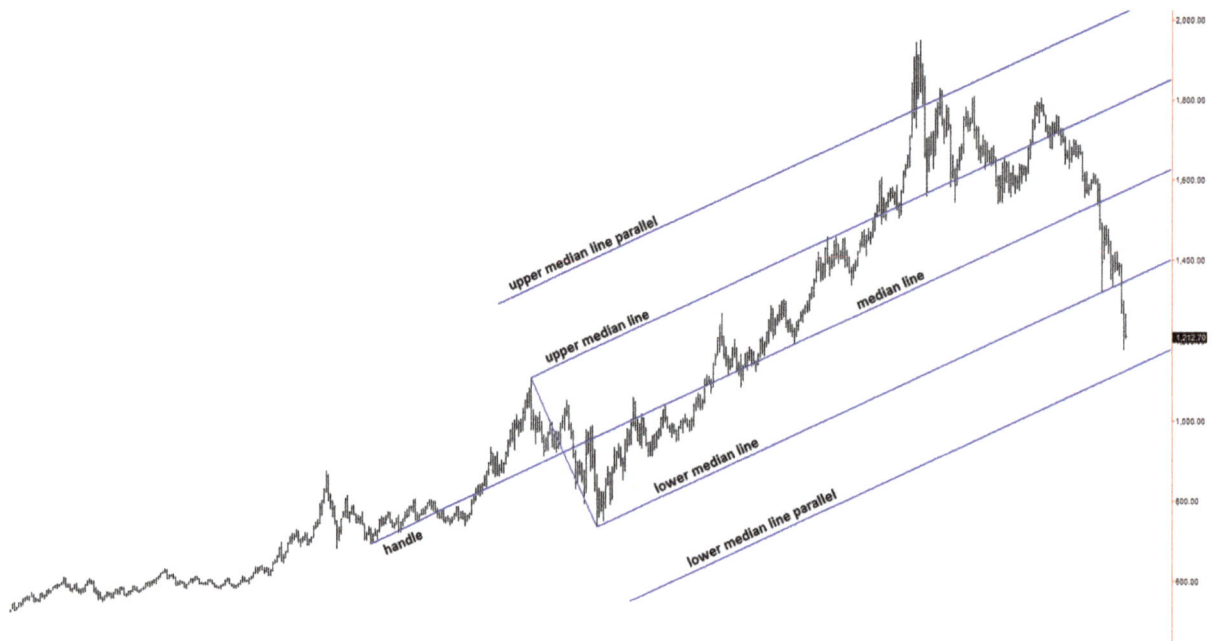

full-size chart available at https://satoritraders.com/andrews-pitchfork/charts

# PART II

## TECHNICAL ANALYSIS

# SUPPORT AND RESISTANCE

In Chart 1 we see price finding support along the bottom of a channel and resistance along the top (1).

Price runs into a horizontal resistance level (2) and then waffles sideways consolidating the recent gains.

After reaching the other side of the channel and finding support (3), price has stored enough energy to punch through the horizontal resistance level and drive all the way to the top of the channel (4) before resting.

Price consolidates after this impulsive upward thrust, and the horizontal level that was acting as resistance provides support on several occasions (5).

In an uptrend resistance becomes support and that is exactly what we are seeing here along the horizontal line. Price tests support along this horizontal level several more times before heading higher and breaking out of the channel (6).

After peaking, price heads lower and drops back into the original channel (7). The top channel line acts as support on the decline and then as resistance as price tests the level from below. Support has become resistance in the downtrend (7).

Price moves lower and tests the channel bottom where support is momentarily found (8). When support fails, price drops out of the channel and then tests the lower channel line from below (9).

Price continues the downward trend inside a narrow channel. The top of this new channel provides another example of how support becomes resistance in a downtrend (10).

Chart 1. Support and resistance

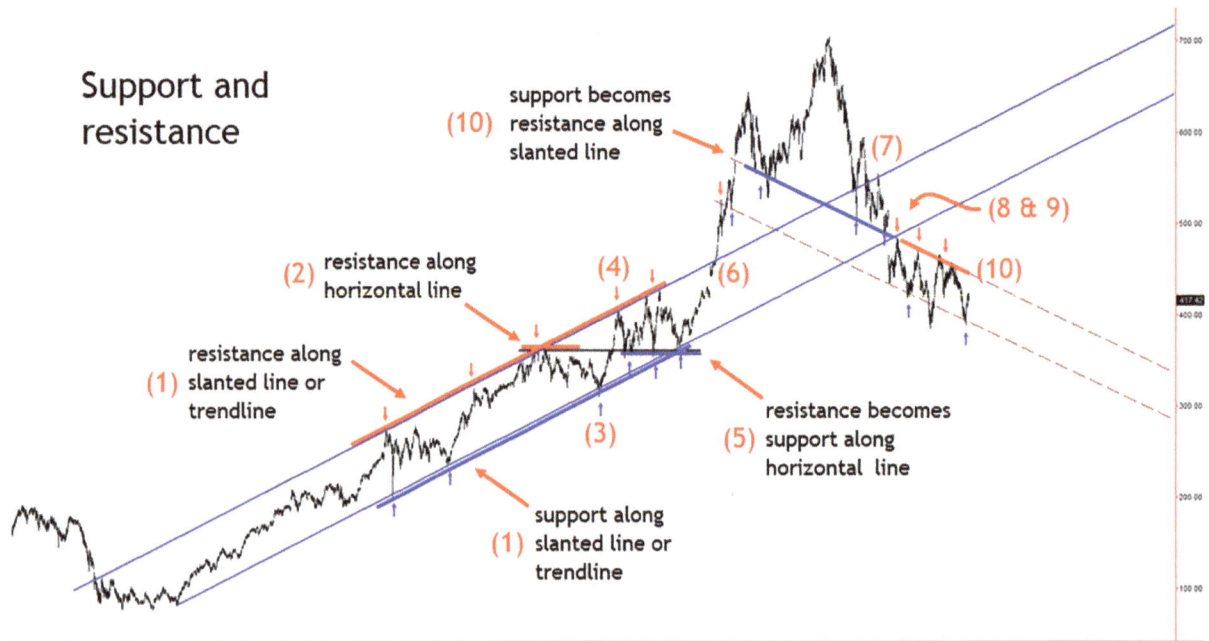

full-size chart available at https://satoritraders.com/andrews-pitchfork/charts

In Chart 1 we see some key concepts in play:

- resistance becomes support in an uptrend

- support becomes resistance in a downtrend

- support and resistance can occur along horizontal or slanted lines

- price is likely to test significant support and resistance levels multiple times

The last bullet above is the key reason we want to pay attention to support and resistance (S/R) levels. After an S/R level is identified, the subsequent tests of that level can give us opportunities to enter and exit the market.

When a test of proven support or resistance fails, we gain valuable information by recognizing that price behavior is changing. We can then adjust our trading strategy for the new market behavior.

Note that drawing S/R levels as thin lines on a chart is somewhat misleading. It would be more accurate to use thick lines to reflect the idea that S/R levels are zones where price behavior will likely be influenced. Charts can quickly become cluttered so we use thin lines and remember that the line represents a zone.

## HORIZONTAL SUPPORT AND RESISTANCE

In Chart 2 horizontal lines are drawn along the tops of prior high points and below the bottoms of prior low points.

There is a great deal of subjectivity in where to draw these lines. Look for areas where resistance turns into support in an uptrend, or support turns into resistance in a downtrend.

If a horizontal line has been tested from both sides it is more likely that the level will provide support and resistance in the future.

Notice how the S/R levels that affected price during the uptrend also influenced price during the downtrend.

Chart 2. Horizontal support and resistance

full-size chart available at https://satoritraders.com/andrews-pitchfork/charts

## ROUND-NUMBER SUPPORT AND RESISTANCE

Round-numbers are another factor that tends to create horizontal S/R levels. The phenomenon is caused by human psychology.

Notice in Chart 3 the resistance that price faced at the $1000 level before breaking higher. The $1400 level is another excellent example of a round-number influencing price.

Chart 3. Round-number support and resistance

full-size chart available at https://satoritraders.com/andrews-pitchfork/charts

## PITCHFORK SUPPORT AND RESISTANCE

In Chart 4 we have a blue Andrews Pitchfork describing a price uptrend. The red Schiff pitchfork describes a price correction or downtrend.

As price moves out of the main channels of a pitchfork we can add the median line parallels to the pitchforks as we see here. The parallels are likely to influence behavior until price starts to oscillate at a different frequency.

Timothy Morge describes the convergence of two fork lines as 'energy points' or 'price magnets' and points out that price can move explosively into and out of these areas. The energy points in Chart 4 are highlighted.

Chart 4. Andrews Pitchfork support and resistance

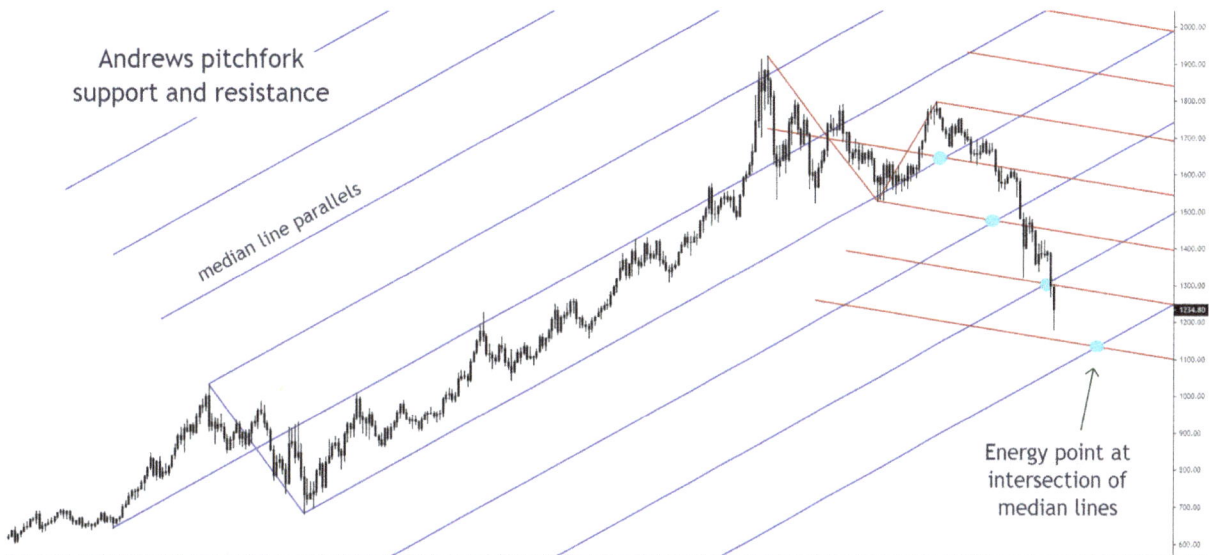

full-size chart available at https://satoritraders.com/andrews-pitchfork/charts

# FIBONACCI RETRACEMENT SUPPORT AND RESISTANCE

When we are looking at a significant price movement it is appropriate to apply a Fibonacci retracement study as we see in Chart 5. This common charting tool is drawn from the start of a price movement (A) to the movement's end (B).

Notice that after price peaked at point B and then plummeted lower, the 23.6% retracement level provided support for a relief rally. Price interacted with this S/R level multiple times before heading decisively lower towards the 38.2% retracement.

The Fibonacci retracement study is most accurate when applied to impulsive price movements. In Chart 5 we are analyzing a multi-year price movement that is not impulsive but the Fibonacci tool is still identifying significant S/R zones.

Note that 50% is not a Fibonacci level although it is included on most Fibonacci drawing tools. The 50% value comes from Dow Theory where it is considered the critical level for determining whether the primary trend will continue after a price pullback.

Chart 5. Fibonacci retracement support and resistance

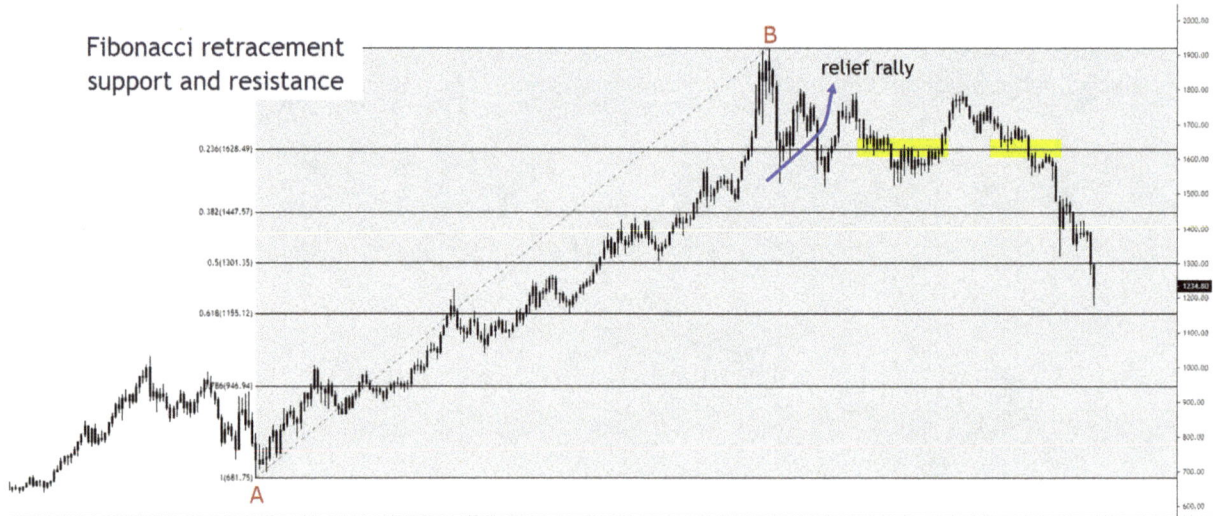

full-size chart available at https://satoritraders.com/andrews-pitchfork/charts

# CONVERGENCE OF SUPPORT AND RESISTANCE

When the same S/R zone is identified by multiple techniques, it is reasonable to expect that the zone will influence price action. We can combine all of the S/R studies into one chart and look for these convergences of support and resistance.

In general, we don't want our charts to look like the cluttered mess in Chart 6. Instead of helping us trade the markets effectively, a chaotic chart like this is more likely to cause confusion and indecision.

In this case we are intentionally creating a messy chart in order to identify where the different types of support and resistance converge.

The yellow highlights show examples of where price has interacted with a convergence of S/R levels during the downtrend.

We can see that the last energy point on this chart coincides with the 61.8% Fibonacci retracement level. It is likely that price will be drawn into the energy point and it is also reasonable to expect some amount of support from the Fibonacci retracement level.

Based on this information we could plan a trading strategy for getting short as price moves into the energy point and then reversing our position as price bounces from the Fibonacci level.

Chart 6. Convergence of support and resistance

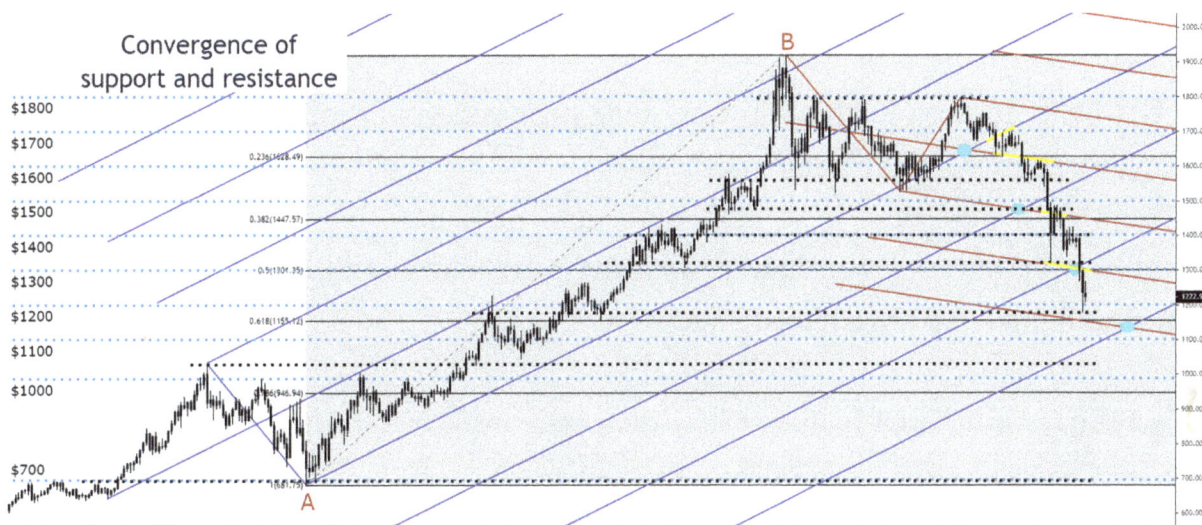

full-size chart available at https://satoritraders.com/andrews-pitchfork/charts

# ENERGY

## PRICE TREND LOSING ENERGY

In Chart 1 the Andrews Pitchfork is describing price action in a long-term uptrend. As the trend matures price forms a triple-top.

The triple-top is already a warning sign that the trend may be ending, but there is an additional clue about what price may do next.

The red ellipses in Chart 1 highlight how each price peak in the triple-top is occurring at a lower level relative to the pitchfork's upper median line.

This failure of price to reach the upper median line is a sign that the uptrend is running out of energy. When price drops below the fork's median line we get another indication that the long-term trend has changed from upwards to downwards.

## Chart 1. Price trend losing energy

full-size chart available at https://satoritraders.com/andrews-pitchfork/charts

# POKEY BARS

'Pokey' bars are price bars that stick out from the bulk of the price action. These distinctive bars indicate extremes in price energy and they frequently provide the pivot points used for drawing Andrews Pitchfork and Fibonacci studies.

On the left side of Chart 2 price action is volatile and we see numerous pokey bars. These high energy price bars suggest that volatility in the market is elevated and we should trade accordingly.

Notice how price behavior changes in the second pitchfork. Instead of forming spike highs and lows (pokey bars) price is forming more rounded tops and bottoms. This suggests that volatility or price energy has decreased and we can adjust our trading strategy accordingly.

## Chart 2. Pokey bars

full-size chart available at https://satoritraders.com/andrews-pitchfork/charts

# STRONG BARS / WEAK BARS

For simplicity we can define a strong price bar as one that closes in the top third of its range. Conversely, a weak price bar closes in the bottom third of its range.

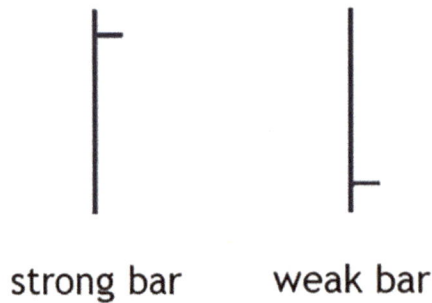

strong bar    weak bar

When a large distance is covered between the high and low of a price bar we can describe it as wide-ranging. Wide-ranging bars are a sign that price energy is elevated.

**Wide-ranging price bars**

full-size chart available at https://satoritraders.com/andrews-pitchfork/charts

If we think of an individual price bar as a battle between buyers and sellers, a wide-ranging price bar tells us that a great battle has occurred and a large amount of energy has been released. These high-energy bars often mark a change in price behavior.

When wide-ranging price bars occur at the start or end of a price movement we tend to get the pokey bars referred to in the previous section. Japanese Candlesticks refer to these wide-ranging bars with the colorful names Dragonfly Doji and Gravestone Doji.

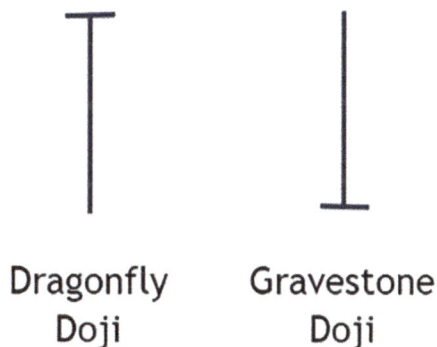

Dragonfly
Doji

Gravestone
Doji

# IMPULSIVE PRICE MOVEMENT

Chart 3 shows price breaking impulsively higher and surpassing two prior price peaks.

In the world of physics (or energy), 'impulsive' typically refers to a significant force being applied for a brief period of time. The force in question is 'significant' because of its ability to cause change and the time period is 'brief' relative to the entire period being studied.

Translating these concepts into the world of price charts we can define 'impulsive' as a significant price change occurring in a short period of time.

Rick Ackerman teaches a method for measuring how impulsive any given move is based on the number of prior peaks surpassed during the move.

In Chart 3 price is ranging mostly sideways before heading higher to 'prior peak #1'. After a shallow correction price bolts higher and surpasses the two prior peaks on its way up which qualifies this move as impulsive.

In addition to surpassing prior peaks we also have numerous high energy price bars occurring on this move. The impulsive move started with two wide-ranging price bars and continued with multiple strong bars.

Chart 3. Impulsive price movement

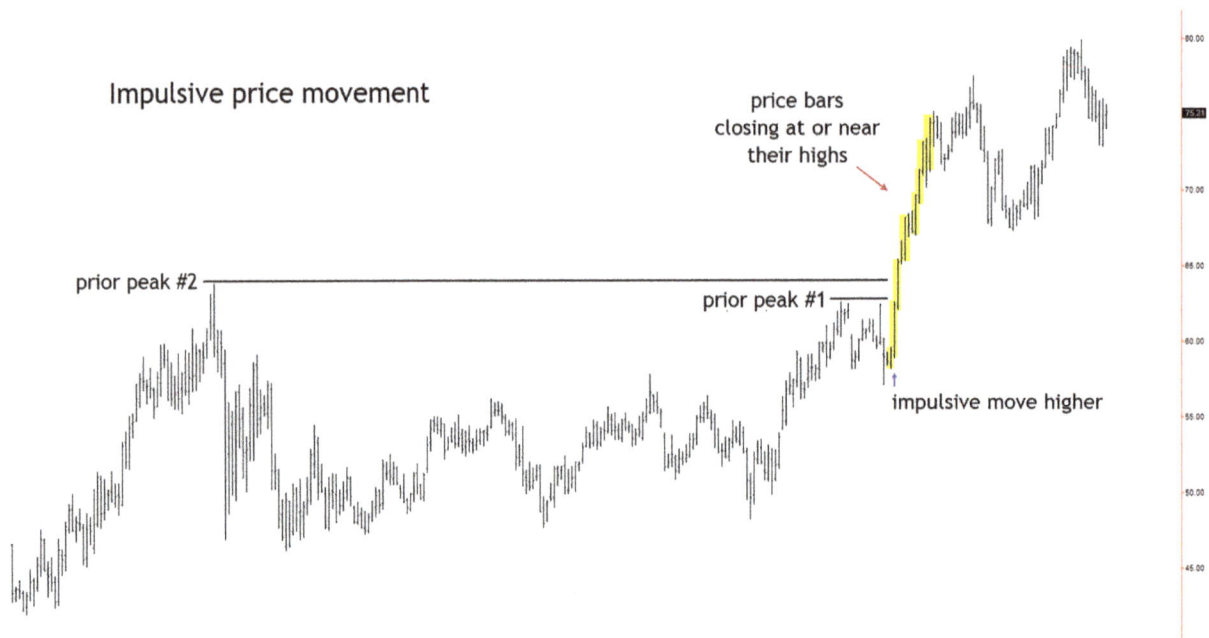

full-size chart available at https://satoritraders.com/andrews-pitchfork/charts

## EXTREME VOLUME

Extreme volume is another sign of high energy. We often see high volume as buyers push price into a peak or when sellers capitulate into a selloff.

In Chart 5 we see price declining as volume increases. There are several bursts of high volume and we get two pokey price bars that correspond with volume spikes.

Each of the high-volume selling spurts could be viewed as capitulation selling but in this example the relentless price decline was not over.

Volume becomes nearly negligible as price shuffles sideways, and then another selloff begins as volume increases dramatically into the final price bottom.

### Chart 5. Extreme volume

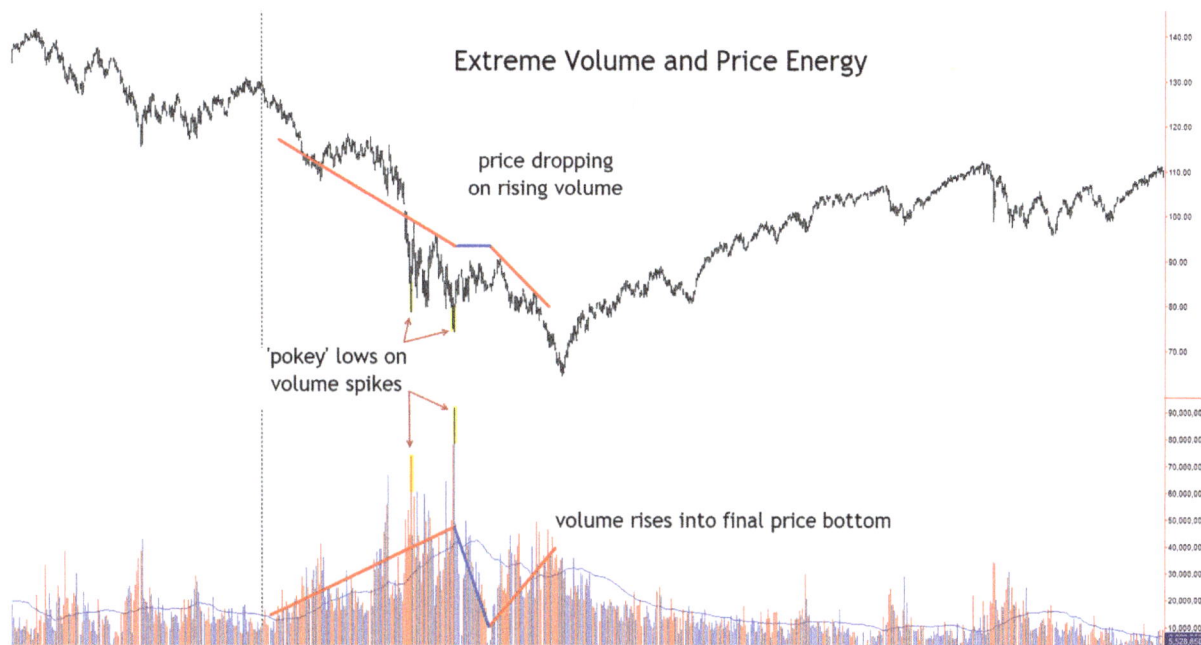

full-size chart available at https://satoritraders.com/andrews-pitchfork/charts

## GAPS

A gap forms in a financial chart when no trading occurs within a certain price range. These gaps are visible displays of stored price energy being released.

There are four types of price gaps and they are demonstrated in Chart 6 and Chart 7.

An exhaustion gap forms at the end of a price move and price typically changes behavior after the gap occurs. A price reversal is possible but a consolidation is more likely since price energy is low. Chart 6 provides an example of price consolidating sideways after an exhaustion gap.

Gaps sometimes occur within a chart pattern and they are referred to as common gaps. In Chart 6 we can see that these common gaps are less significant than the exhaustion and breakaway gaps.

A breakaway gap occurs when price breaks out of a congestion pattern. In Chart 6 price restores its energy as it shuffles sideways within the trading range. The stored energy then gets released to the downside in a breakaway gap and price continues its downtrend.

Chart 6. Gaps

full-size chart available at https://satoritraders.com/andrews-pitchfork/charts

Chart 7 provides an example of runaway gaps.

After price finds support along the median line of the Andrews Pitchfork in Chart 7 we get a wide-ranging price bar that closes almost at its high. Price then gaps higher to another wide-ranging bar that closes almost on its high point. Price gaps higher yet again and forms an extremely wide-ranging bar as it pushes through the pitchfork's upper median line.

Runaway gaps indicate that price energy is extremely elevated. In this example we have both the runaway gaps and the wide-ranging price bars telling us that price is heading higher and that is exactly what happened.

Chart 7. Runaway gaps

full-size chart available at https://satoritraders.com/andrews-pitchfork/charts

# FIBONACCI RETRACEMENT

Fibonacci retracement assumes that markets will partially retrace a price movement and then resume moving in the original direction.

## PRICE PULLBACK IN AN UPTREND

One of the ways we can use the Fibonacci retracement tool is to help us pick an entry point in an ongoing uptrend.

Chart 1 provides an example where the price of Gold futures has broken above the $1750 level. Let's assume we want to take a long position in the market and we are planning our trading strategy.

Knowing that financial markets breathe in and out, we want to let price pullback and provide us with a cheaper entry point. The Fibonacci retracement tool gives us a way to predict where a price pullback is likely to find support before reversing higher.

In the chart we apply the Fibonacci retracement tool to the price movement from point A to point B and focus on the 23.6%, 38.2%, and 50% retracement levels (highlighted).

Notice that we have convergences of support at the 38.2% and 50% levels. At 38.2% we have the lower median line of the blue Andrews Pitchfork and 50% is just below a horizontal S/R zone.

## Chart 1. Fibonacci retracement in an uptrend

full-size chart available at https://satoritraders.com/andrews-pitchfork/charts

Price has already completed a 23.6% retracement and turned higher so the pullback may be over already.

A breakout trader might consider this shallow pullback a successful retest of the breakout level and take a long position in the market with a stop below the 23.6% level.

More conservative traders will wait for price to pull back to the 38.2% or 50% levels where the convergences of support can be tested.

Having well-defined and written trading rules simplifies our decision-making process in a situation like this. If our trading plan includes breakout strategies we can follow our corresponding rules. If our trading plan requires a minimum 38.2% pullback we sit on our hands until that occurs.

## COMMON FIBONACCI LEVELS

The retracement levels commonly seen in real-life price behavior are 23.6%, 38.2%, 50%, and 61.8%.

A 23.6% retracement is very shallow and indicates continuing strength in the prevailing trend. Typically we are looking for price to reverse in the 38.2% to 61.8% zone.

Most Fibonacci retracement tools include the 50% level even though 50% is not based on a Fibonacci number. The 50% level comes from Dow Theory where it is considered the critical level for determining whether the primary trend will continue after a price pullback.

## RELIEF RALLY IN A DOWNTREND

The same Fibonacci concepts apply when we want to take a short position in a downward trending market. In that case we apply the Fibonacci retracement tool to a significant downward price movement and the retracement levels show us where a bear market rally is likely to run out of energy and return to the downward price trend.

Chart 2 shows Brent Oil completing a 61.8% price retracement before rolling-over and resuming its downward trend. The 61.8% Fibonacci level was coincident with a convergence of resistance provided by the median line of the modified-Schiff pitchfork and the horizontal S/R level.

The convergence of resistance identified a price level where the relief rally was likely to run out of energy, and obviously that is what happened.

## Chart 2. Fibonacci retracement in a downtrend

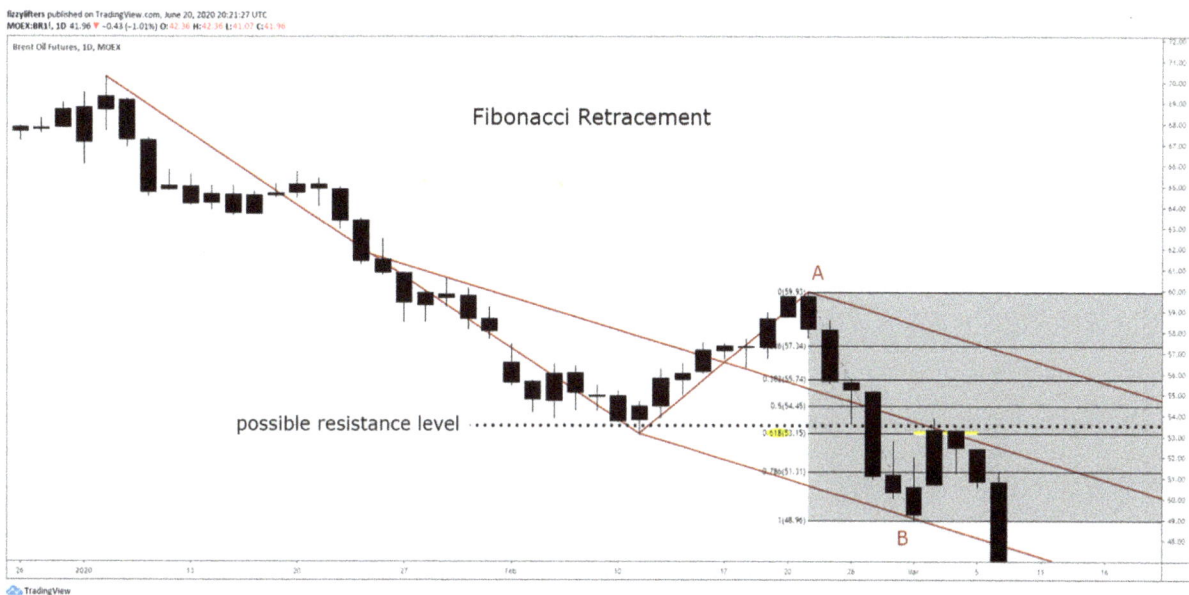

full-size chart available at https://satoritraders.com/andrews-pitchfork/charts

# FIBONACCI EXTENSION

The Fibonacci extension tool lets us predict when a price movement is likely to end.

Using this information we can determine price targets for a potential trade or evaluate whether a price movement has completed.

## FORECASTING PRICE TARGETS

In this example we are range-trading the stock in Chart 1 and want to manage our latest long entry. After entering our position at the bottom of the channel, price has catapulted higher in an impulsive move.

Chart 1. Range-trading example

full-size chart available at https://satoritraders.com/andrews-pitchfork/charts

We can apply the Fibonacci extension tool to the impulsive move and determine where the price advance is likely to run out of energy. Based on this information we can then set a profit target that has a high probability of being reached.

In Chart 2 we can see that the A-to-B move consists of four price bars. The first bar at A has a long bullish tail and closed on its high. Next come two wide-ranging price bars that close on their highs. These three bars are demonstrating that price energy is high. Price then gaps up to point B before retreating lower.

By applying the Fibonacci tool to the A-B-C price pivots we get the target at point D which is the 100% extension level. This is a level where the current price movement is likely to run out of energy.

For this trading example we notice that the predicted price target occurs below the top of the channel we are trading. We may want to take profits at that point or tighten the stop on our trade to protect profits.

Chart 2. Fibonacci extension of A-B-C move

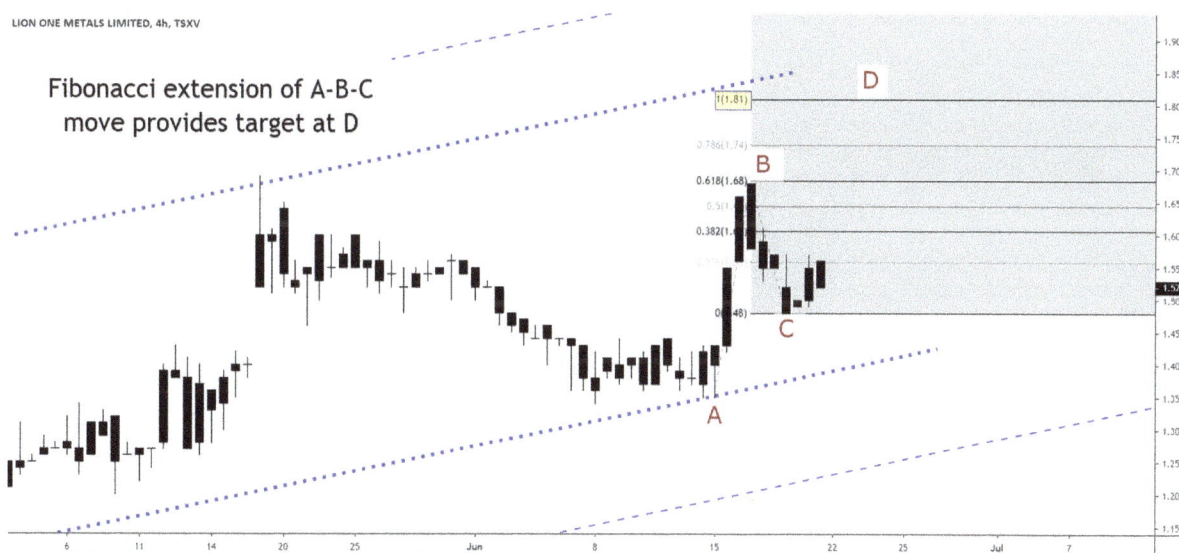

full-size chart available at https://satoritraders.com/andrews-pitchfork/charts

The Fibonacci extension tool is most accurate when it is applied to impulsive price movements. In Chart 2 the A-to-B move qualifies as impulsive based on the high-energy price bars and exhaustion price gap.

Rick Ackerman teaches specific techniques for using the Fibonacci extension tool. His methods are highly accurate and include well-defined rules for determining when the results of the Fibonacci extension can, and cannot be relied on.

## EVALUATING PRICE MOVEMENT

The Fibonacci extension tool can be applied to an impulsive price movement as part of evaluating price behavior and preparing a financial forecast. Instead of finding a price target in the future we want to determine if a price target has already been reached.

Based on the principles for using the Fibonacci extension tool we can expect price to run out of energy when it reaches the D target (100% extension) and either reverse or consolidate.

In this example we will apply these principles to forecast whether the price of the stock in Chart 3 is likely to continue higher.

Chart 3. Forecasting price behavior

full-size chart available at https://satoritraders.com/andrews-pitchfork/charts

In Chart 4 we see that the individual price bars in the A-to-B move are not particularly high-energy. The overall move, however, qualifies as impulsive because it covers a large distance in a short period of time. We will assume that it is appropriate to apply the Fibonacci extension tool to this price movement.

Applying the Fibonacci study to our chart we find that our D target lies well above the current price level. Although there is a confluence of resistance that has to be overcome, it is likely that price will push higher and ultimately reach D.

With the knowledge we have gained from the Fibonacci tool we can now plan a breakout trade with a price target at the D level.

Chart 4. Fibonacci extension of A-B-C move

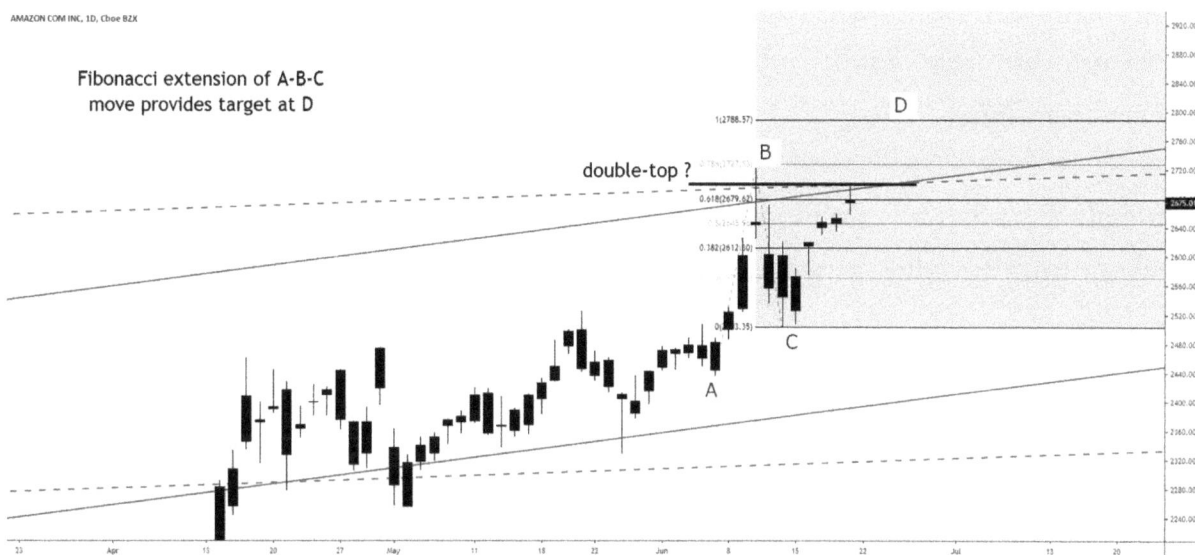

full-size chart available at https://satoritraders.com/andrews-pitchfork/charts

# VOLUME

There are only five pieces of fundamental data on any given price bar: open, high, low, close (OHLC), and volume.

We can use volume to confirm the OHLC information and increase the accuracy of our price action trading.

In general, chart patterns are more reliable when they occur on high volume. For example, a breakout from a trading range has more significance if it occurs on high volume.

A volume spike often marks the end of a downtrend as some traders capitulate and others reposition for a new uptrend. The high-volume selling marks a shift in market sentiment from bearish to bullish.

These are the key aspects of volume behavior to consider:

- High volume confirms a price move

- Volume increases as price moves in the direction of the primary trend

- When volume rises as price rises the primary trend is up

- When volume rises as price declines the primary trend is down

- Volume spikes often mark the end of downtrends

# VOLUME CONFIRMS PRICE MOVEMENT

In Chart 1 price is clearly in an uptrend and there appears to be a breakout occurring.

Before taking a long position in this stock we want to verify that volume behavior is consistent with an uptrend.

We start by identifying the horizontal S/R level and pennant pattern. This clarifies the price action and allows us to focus on volume behavior.

Volume is rising as price rises towards the S/R level. This is the behavior we would expect to see in an uptrend.

As price surges impulsively through the S/R level volume surges as well, then peaks and falls off during the sideways consolidation which forms the pennant pattern.

In the most recent action volume is rising again as price breaks out through the top of the pennant. Price and volume rising together tells us that the trend is upwards.

This breakout appears to be legitimate and we can see that this stock is exhibiting multiple signs of high energy. We can now implement our trading rules for entering a breakout trade.

Chart 1. Volume confirms price movement

full-size chart available at https://satoritraders.com/andrews-pitchfork/charts

# VOLUME SPIKES AND CAPITULATION SELLING

In Chart 2 price is waffling sideways in a trading range. Long-term investors may be frustrated by this kind of price action but nimble traders can make a healthy living with a $6 price range like this.

As traders the volume behavior in this example increases our confidence in taking our next long position at current price levels. We know that downtrends often end with capitulation selling and that appears to be happening now.

In addition to the surge in volume we have price testing a confluence of support.

While price can do anything it wants, there is a high probability that a price reversal is about to occur in this stock.

As traders we can now implement our trading rules for entering a price reversal within a trading range.

Chart 2. Volume spikes and capitulation selling

full-size chart available at https://satoritraders.com/andrews-pitchfork/charts

# INDICATORS

There are only two types of fundamental data when we look at a chart: price (OHLC) and volume. If we break price down to its components (open, high, low, close), there are five pieces of fundamental data when we include volume.

With only five pieces of fundamental data available, how do we explain the hundreds of different indicators that we can apply to our charts?

In a nutshell, these indicators *derive* additional information about price behavior by using the five pieces of fundamental data.

That's not a bad objective but each derivation of the fundamental data takes us farther away from the actual price action and introduces a time lag between the price action and the indicator.

## MACD – 4 LEVELS OF DERIVED DATA

As an example, let's consider the MACD indicator which is based on one slow and one fast moving average of price. Since price is our fundamental data, the moving averages become the first derivative of the underlying data.

The MACD line is a difference between the two moving averages so it represents the second derivative of the price data. The MACD signal line is a moving average of the MACD line so that gives us a third derivative.

Taking the difference between the MACD and MACD signal lines gives us the MACD Histogram as the fourth derivative of the fundamental data.

## ARE INDICATORS USEFUL?

We might question the value of any information provided by the fourth derivative of fundamental data, especially when the derived information lags in time behind the fundamental data.

In general, we want to base our trading decisions on fundamental data which means the price action itself and the volume that occurs during the period of interest.

Indicators can be useful, however. Even with their limitations, they can help us confirm the price action and provide us with buy/sell signals.

Indicators also allow us to screen price charts when we are looking for high probability trading opportunities. Most trading and charting platforms provide screeners which include filters based on MACD and Stochastics.

If we are looking for long trades, for example, we can screen for stocks where Slow Stochastics is elevated (high price energy) and both MACD lines are greater than zero (primary price trend is up).

When we choose to use indicators it is important to keep two things in mind:

- Indicators show us derived data, not fundamental data
- Indicators lag the price action

## THE ULTIMATE INDICATOR

There are several traps we can fall into when it comes to the vast world of indicators.

The first trap is the illusive search for the 'ultimate' indicator. With numerous indicators to choose from this search could easily take a lifetime. Besides the commonly available indicators, an infinite number of custom indicators can be created using advanced trading / charting platforms like Tradestation.

Another trap is thinking that more is better – i.e., if one indicator is good then surely two are better. The problem is that two indicators rarely provide the same signal so we end up trying to interpret conflicting messages from multiple indicators.

Ideally our trading plan will define the specific entry and exit criteria we will use for trading. Consistent, long-term profitability for most traders involves following a well-defined set of trading rules. Successful discretionary (seat-of-the-pants) traders are rare.

In an attempt to find the perfect indicator or integrate signals from multiple indicators an aspiring trader may never reach the point of creating a trading plan and actually taking action in the markets.

To avoid these pitfalls we can choose to rely primarily on fundamental data (price and volume) while supplementing this data occasionally with just one or two indicators.

The most useful common indicators for price action trading are MACD and Slow Stochastics as shown in Chart 1. Volume is fundamental data although it is often displayed at the bottom of a chart like other indicators.

## Chart 1. MACD, Slow Stochastics and Volume

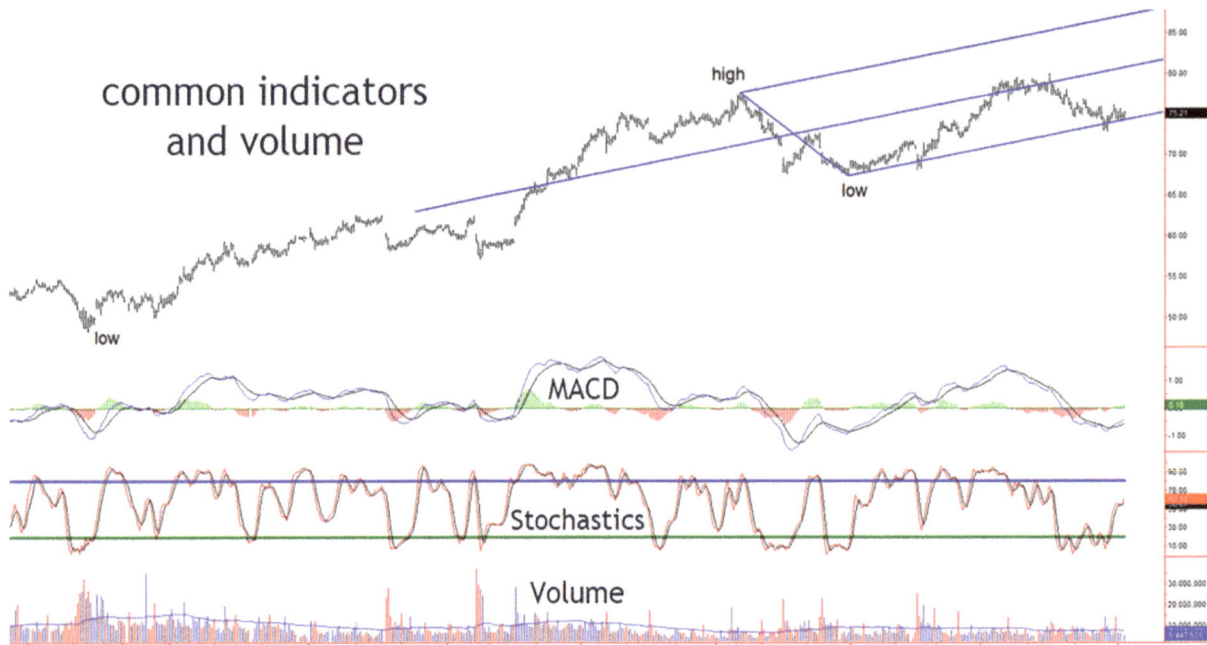

common indicators
and volume

full-size chart available at https://satoritraders.com/andrews-pitchfork/charts

# LAGGING VS LEADING

All indicators are lagging because they present derived information based on something that happened in the past: the open, high, low, close (OHLC) and volume that occurred on previous price bars.

Any signal provided by an indicator has to lag the current price action because of this fundamental dependency on historic data.

# VOLUME AS AN INDICATOR

Volume is sometimes referred to as a leading indicator because it can predict trend reversals. This idea is flawed, however, for two reasons:

1.  Volume is fundamental data so it cannot be an 'indicator' as we are using the term.

2.  Some trends end with a volume spike, some trends end with a gradual decline in volume.

Because volume behavior isn't consistent at the end of a trend, trying to use volume as an indicator makes our trading decisions harder, not easier.

## RULES FOR USING INDICATORS MUST BE CONSISTENT

If we were going to define what an indicator is or isn't, one of our tenets would be that the rules for using an indicator must be consistent.

For example, the MACD line moving below the MACD signal line is always considered a sell signal. There are no market conditions where we are supposed to interpret this crossover as a buy signal.

Volume wouldn't qualify as an indicator under this definition because there are no consistent rules for interpreting volume.

## PREDICTIVE TOOLS

In contrast to indicators which help us confirm price action and provide us with buy/sell signals, we have a few predictive tools we can use to determine in advance where price is likely headed.

These tools let us determine in advance where support and resistance levels are likely to occur. We can then build our trading plan around that price forecast.

The predictive tools are Andrews Pitchfork and the Fibonacci Retracement / Extension studies covered in other sections of this material.

# MACD

Gerald Appel developed the Moving Average Convergence-Divergence (MACD) momentum oscillator in the late 1970's. As its name suggests, the indicator is based on two moving averages and the convergence and divergence of those moving averages.

The MACD indicator provides information about both momentum and trend. A rising MACD line indicates that price momentum is increasing to the upside. When the MACD line is falling price momentum is increasing to the downside.

Trend is determined by the MACD line and its position relative to the indicator's centerline. When the MACD line is above the centerline price is likely trending up with the opposite behavior likely if the MACD line falls below the centerline.

The MACD-Histogram was developed by Thomas Aspray in the mid-1980s to anticipate signals in the MACD.

## Chart 1. MACD terminology

full-size chart available at https://satoritraders.com/andrews-pitchfork/charts

# MACD Trading Signals

The MACD indicator provides several signals:

- Buy/sell as the MACD line crosses the MACD signal line

- Warning signal when the price and MACD trends diverge (price rising as MACD falls or vice-versa)

# MACD Crossover Buy/Sell Signals

Signal line crossovers are the most common MACD signals.

A buy signal occurs when the MACD line crosses the signal line to the upside. A sell signal is issued when the MACD line crosses back below the signal line.

These signals are most effective when MACD levels are either overbought or oversold. Because MACD is an unbounded indicator, overbought and oversold are only meaningful relative to previous highs and lows in the indicator.

MACD becomes overbought when it reaches and/or exceeds the level of the previous MACD high. Conversely, MACD becomes oversold when it reaches and/or exceeds the level of the previous MACD low.

MACD crossover signals can be used as entry/exit triggers for trading or as confirmation of a suspected change in trend direction. Like all indicators, MACD lags the price action so we may already be in a trade before the crossover signal occurs.

Chart 2. MACD trading signals

full-size chart available at https://satoritraders.com/andrews-pitchfork/charts

# MACD DIVERGENCE

Divergences between MACD and price can serve as a warning that price behavior is about to change. This signal isn't reliable enough to use as part of a trading rule but it is another piece of information we can glean from a chart if we are paying attention.

In Chart 3 price rallies to two new all-time-highs (highlighted) after MACD issues a sell signal. Some traders will exit on the MACD sell signal, others will hold their positions with price targets at the upper median line (UML) extension of the modified-Schiff pitchfork.

As this rally unfolds, price reaches the UML extension twice while MACD heads steadily lower. Pitchfork traders have two opportunities to take full or partial profits.

Assuming a trader is aware of it, the divergence between price and MACD might be an influencing factor when deciding between a partial exit or a full exit.

Chart 3. MACD divergence

full-size chart available at https://satoritraders.com/andrews-pitchfork/charts

## MACD as a Trend Indicator

Chart 4 demonstrates how the MACD indicator helps us assess trend.

When the MACD line crosses the centerline on its way up price is entering a bullish phase where the primary trend is likely to be upwards. Most traders will be looking for opportunities to get long.

The MACD line crossing below the centerline of the indicator puts price into a bearish phase. With price in a bear phase the primary trend is likely to be downward and short trades are usually the objective.

There are times when a market waffles sideways or whipsaws back-and-forth. As traders we can adapt to the prevalent conditions or look for markets that better suit our trading strategy.

Chart 4. MACD as a trend indicator

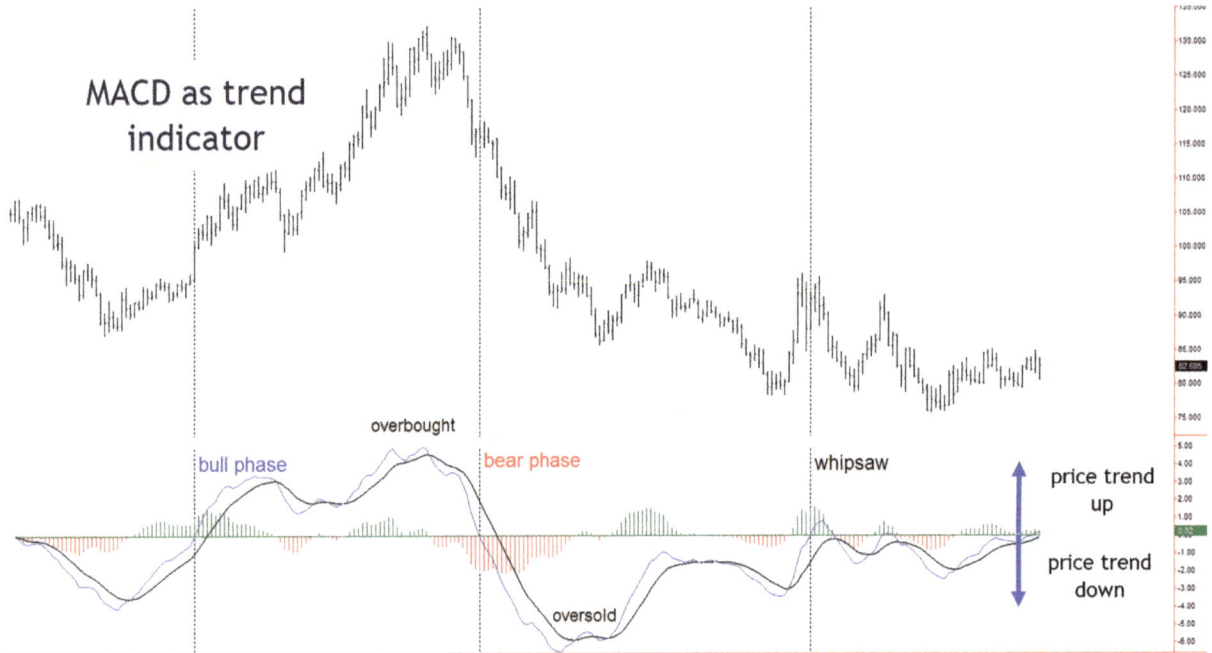

full-size chart available at https://satoritraders.com/andrews-pitchfork/charts

# SLOW STOCHASTICS

The Slow Stochastics indicator was developed by George C. Lane in the late 1950's with the intention of measuring the momentum of price.

Mr. Lane described his indicator this way: "Stochastics measures the momentum of price. If you visualize a rocket going up in the air – before it can turn down, it must slow down. Momentum always changes direction before price."

Chart 1 demonstrates this rocket concept. After the Stochastics indicator rolls over and heads lower, price (the rocket) runs out of energy and ultimately turns lower.

Chart 1. Slow Stochastics and price energy

full-size chart available at https://satoritraders.com/andrews-pitchfork/charts

When we talk about an individual price bar (e.g., pokey, wide-ranging, strong, weak) as an indication of price energy, the time frame we are referring to is obviously just a single bar. When we refer to the Slow Stochastics indicator we are talking about price energy over a series of bars. In both cases it is the same concept of price energy being applied to different time frames.

Price energy within an individual bar is considered strong when the bar closes within its upper third. A weak price bar closes in its lower third.

With the Stochastics indicator price energy is strong (high) above the 80 level and weak (low) below the 20 level.

## SLOW STOCHASTICS AS A MEASURE OF PRICE ENERGY

As traders we are looking for directional price movement. Up or down doesn't particularly matter as long as there is movement.

Upward price movement requires energy. In the absence of energy price falls. If we want to make money trading the financial markets, being able to measure price energy is an important skill.

In our investigation of price energy we have looked at Andrews Pitchfork, strong and weak price bars, 'pokey bars', wide-ranging bars, impulsive price moves, price gaps, and volume spikes. These energy clues are readily available but it takes time to draw market structure on a chart and interpret individual price bars.

The Slow Stochastics indicator gives us a quick way to measure the price energy of a potential trading vehicle before taking the time required to focus on individual price bars and chart patterns.

If we are looking for short trades we can focus on charts where price energy is elevated but waning.

When our trading strategy emphasizes long trades we can use the Slow Stochastics indicator to screen for vehicles where price energy is rising, or already elevated.

## BOUND INDICATOR

As a bound indicator Stochastics always stays in the range between 0 and 100 making it easy to identify high energy (overbought) and low energy (oversold) conditions.

It is important to remember that range bound indicators can remain overbought and oversold for extended periods in trending markets.

# REFERENCES

## TIMOTHY MORGE

BOOK:    **Trading with Median Lines: Mapping the Markets**
by Timothy Morge
ISBN-10: 0972982906
ISBN-13: 978-0972982900
Publisher: Blackthorne Capital, Inc. (2003)


## RICK ACKERMAN

TRAINING:    **The Hidden Pivot Course**
https://www.rickackerman.com/hidden-pivot-course/

WEBSITE:    https://www.rickackerman.com/

# RESOURCES

Full-size versions of the charts in this book are available at:

    https://satoritraders.com/andrews-pitchfork/charts

For examples of applied Andrews Pitchfork strategy and Technical analysis visit:

**Satori Traders YouTube channel**:

    https://www.youtube.com/channel/UCGwy3eroG1DuxOwf1f5S7yg/videos

**Satori Traders website**:

    https://satoritraders.com/

For regular insight into the financial markets using Andrews Pitchforks sign up:

**Satori Traders free newsletter**:

    https://satoritraders.com/#MarketPulse

www.ingramcontent.com/pod-product-compliance
Lightning Source LLC
Chambersburg PA
CBHW052350210326
41597CB00038B/6320